# Profiles in Oriental Diagnosis

## Volume I
### The Renaissance

## By Alex Jack
### Foreword by Michio Kushi

## One Peaceful World Press
### Becket, Massachusetts

*From food are born all creatures.*
*They live upon food, they are dissolved in food.*
*Food is the chief of all things, the universal medicine. . . .*
*I am this world and I eat this world.*
*Who knows this, knows.*
*—Upanishads*

*In memory of my father, Homer A. Jack*

One Peaceful World Press
P.O. Box 10, Leland Road
Becket, MA 01223, U.S.A.
Telephone (413) 623-2322, Fax (413) 623-8827

First Edition: November 1995
10 9 8 7 6 5 4 3 2 1

ISBN 1–882984–16–1
Printed in U.S.A.

One Peaceful World is an international information network and
friendship society devoted to the realization of one healthy, peaceful
world. Activities include educational and spiritual tours, assemblies
and forums, international food aid and development, and publishing.
Membership is $30/year for individuals and $50 for families and includes an annual subscription to the *One Peaceful World Newsletter* .
For information, contact OPW at the above address.

The Kushi Institute offers ongoing classes and seminars including classes and workshops on Oriental Diagnosis. For information,
contact: Kushi Institute, Box 7, Becket, MA 01223, (413) 623-5741. Fax
413-623-8827.

# Contents

*"There is properly no history; only biography."*
— Emerson

# Foreword

The principal tool of Oriental diagnosis is physiognomy, which the dictionary defines as "the art of judging character and disposition from the features of the face or the form and lineaments of the body generally." The secret of diagnostic skill is to recognize the signs of a particular set of changes before they become serious—to see visual clues on the face or in the eyes that stones are developing in the kidneys, that the heart is expanding, or that a tumor is developing—even before these symptoms bring pain or discomfort. Then corrective action—principally diet, but also environment and lifestyle—can be taken to maintain usual good health. The primary compass that we use in Oriental diagnosis to evaluate ourselves, other people, and the world around us is yang and yin—the spiral forces of heaven and earth, centripetality and centrifugality, contraction and expansion that make up and govern all things.

Complementary to this is Nine Star Ki, the system of astrology and directionology underlying ancient cosmologies. From yin and yang, first five and then nine archetypal stages of energy are generated, giving us a more precise tool of analysis. In the macrobiotic community, we use the Five Transformations and Nine Star Ki to observe and understand daily life, including our relationships with other people, to determine the best directions to travel (or avoid), and to predict the weather and monthly energy flow. For very difficult decisions, we meditate or consult the *I Ching*—the ancient Chinese *Book of Change* based on a deep understanding of yin and yang and Nine Star Ki—for advice and guidance.

Over the years, these methods also have been employed to understand cycles of social destiny. George Ohsawa introduced dietetics in his short biographies of Ben Franklin, young Gandhi, and others that he wrote for Japanese schoolchildren at the end of World War II.

5

In my lecture in the 1960s and 1970s, I developed the Spiral of History (*see p. 137*) to describe the marvelous order and unity to unfolding human evolution, chart the accelerating rise and fall of civilizations, and describe an era of peace and harmony that may begin about A.D. 2100 when the North Star reaches its zenith and the planet's energy field becomes more highly charged. In *One Peaceful World* (St. Martin's Press, 1987), Alex and I applied these methods to the subject of war and peace, reviewed the history of human culture from ancient to modern times, and outlined the probable stages of development that modern civilization will pass through in the 21st century.

Nature governs our daily life. The foods we eat speak through us with a characteristic voice and appear in our thoughts, features, and gestures. From a painting, a letter, a signature, a photograph, a voice recording, and other autobiographical fragments, we can discern the essence of a person's character and destiny. In *Profiles in Oriental Diagnosis*, Alex presents case histories of several great Renaissance figures and shows how diet, environment, and lifestyle, as well as celestial and terrestrial Ki flow, shaped their health and judgment, their accomplishments and legacy. From paintings and drawings, engravings and sculptures, poems and journals, he observes the physiognomies of his subjects and—with the help of Nine Star Ki and the *I Ching*—deduces what they ate, how they acted, what they thought, and the source of their inspiration and genius.

*Profiles in Oriental Diagnosis* reveals the hidden spirals and currents of life, history, and art. Blending science and myth, literature and medicine, this book is a breakthrough in understanding the creative geniuses of our age and the world in which we live.

In the coming century, humanity will perfect physiognomy, dietetics, Nine Star Ki, the *I Ching*, the art of placement, transmutation, and other tools of life to inaugurate a bright new era of endless self-development, family harmony, and planetary peace. *Profiles in Oriental Diagnosis* gives wings to that hope.

Michio Kushi
Brookline, Massachusetts
June 1, 1995

# Preface

Life moves in a spiral. In the Spiral of History, our present society occupies the same stage as the Renaissance, and the Renaissance is an apt entry point for our study of modern life and thought. There are also recurrent spirals in everyone's personal life, and the creative personalities examined in this book continue to weave through mine. From a young age, I was attracted to Leonardo's work, especially his left-handness which I share, and his ability to synthesize art and science. In my youthful wanderings, I spent many hours atop the great Cathedral in Florence (associated with Dante, Leonardo, and other poets and artists) meditating on the nature of life and fell under the hypnotic gaze of the *Mona Lisa* in the Louvre in Paris.

My father's ancestors may have been engulfed in the wave of religious persecution against liberal Christians, Jews, and Muslims that swept through Europe at the time of Columbus's enterprise. From my grandparents, I inherited some souvenirs of the 1893 Columbian Exposition. The spirit of the World's Parliament of Religions, held in Chicago (my hometown) as part of the 400th anniversary celebration of Columbus' landing, marked the first global meeting of Eastern and Western faiths and became an inspiration for my father's career as a Unitarian minister and crusader for racial and religious toleration. As the subject of her first book report in grade school, my Russian daughter chose Christopher Columbus.

Throughout my life, like many lovers of poetry and literature, I have been attracted to the works of Shakespeare. My grandfather, Rev. David Rhys Williams, was deeply involved in Shakespearean authorship studies and, when I was twelve, I painted a picture for him of Christopher Marlowe, his candidate for the laurels. My grandmother's ancestors lived in Fakenham, a small town in England, and I like to imagine them attending a production of *Hamlet* or *A Midsummer Night's Dream* in London or on one of Shakespeare's country tours.

Originally, this study of creativity and modern thought was conceived as a single book. However, it has taken on a life of its own and is likely to extend to several volumes. Future subjects will include Descartes, Newton, Jefferson, Darwin, Pasteur, Lincoln, Marx, Freud, Einstein, Madame Curie, Picasso, Mao, Martin Luther King, and other men and women. A study of these giants is a prelude to developing a new model of the cosmos. Just as the Renaissance began with the rediscovery of the classics and reinterpretation of the received wisdom of the past, so our new era will commence with a new comprehensive interpretation of the creators of the modern mind. In the course of our journey, we shall trace the decline and fall of the unifying principle in the agrarian, industrial, and scientific revolutions, as well as review current ruling myths, including evolution and the survival of the fittest, the immutability of the periodic table of elements, the big bang theory of the origin of the universe, DNA and the genetic code, and the cybernetic model of change.

Today all systems in society are collapsing, not only the family, church, and state, but also modern medicine, science, psychology, and the arts. Over the next generation, the seeds of a new cosmology, biology, chemistry, physics, astronomy, politics, economics, and spiritual orientation will blossom. Our planet will undergo a new Copernican Revolution with the logarithmic spiral or helix—the universal image of balance, harmony, and interconnectedness—at its center. To this end, this series of volumes is dedicated.

*Profiles in Oriental Diagnosis* is written for the general reader, and no previous familiarity with Oriental diagnosis, Nine Star Ki, or the *I Ching* is needed. However, an Appendix with recommended reading is provided for those who wish to study these subjects further. Classes in Oriental diagnosis and macrobiotic philosophy and health care offered by the Kushi Institute are also highly advised.

In seeing this project to fruition, the author would like to thank Michio Kushi for his endless inspiration and guidance; his wife, Gale, for her love, nourishing cooking, and copyediting; his children, Masha and Jon, for their constant reminder of what is really important in life; his mother, Esther, for her loving encouragement; and his other family, friends, students, and colleagues.

Alex Jack
Becket, Massachusetts
August 5, 1995

# Leonardo
# Da Vinci

*"A good painter has essentially two things to represent: a person and that person's state of mind."*
—Leonardo, Notebooks

*"If you would be healthy, observe this advice:*
*Eat only when hungry, and let light fare suffice.*
*Chew all your food well, and this rule always follow:*
*Well cooked and simple be all that you swallow.*
*On leaving the table, a good posture keep,*
*And after your luncheon do not yield to sleep,*
*Let little and often be your rule for wine,*
*But not between meals or when waiting to dine.*
—Leonardo, Notebooks

*"Supreme happiness will be the cause of misery and the perfection of wisdom the occasion of folly."*
—Leonardo, Notebooks

*"Leonardo is the Hamlet of art history, whom each of us must recreate for himself . . . "*
—Kenneth Clark, Leonardo da Vinci

*"While Cristobal Colón [Columbus] ventured across the vast expanse of the ocean into the unknown, it was left to Leonardo to be the greatest explorer of something closer at hand, the human body itself."*
—A. Richard Turner, Inventing Leonardo

*"Leonardo was notable for his quiet peaceableness and his avoidance of all antagonism and controversy. He was gentle and kindly to everyone; declined, it is said to eat meat . . [But it did] not stop him from devising the cruellest offensive weapons and entering the service of Cesare Borgia as chief military engineer."*
—Freud, Leonardo da Vinci and a Memory of His Childhood

---

*Overleaf:* Mona Lisa, *begun in 1503 (Louvre, Paris)*

## Leonardo da Vinci
# A Portrait of Leonardo

 ruly heaven sometimes sends us those who represent not only humanity but also divinity itself, so that, observing these models, we can draw nearer in spirit and excellence to the sublimities of heaven. Physical beauty never adequately praised, the more than infinite grace in every action, the great strength with dexterity, the spirit and courage, always regal and magnanimous."

Thus Leonardo da Vinci (1452-1519) was described about thirty years after his death by his biographer Giorgi Vasari. Since then, while the colors of *The Last Supper, Mona Lisa,* and his other masterpieces have continued to fade, Leonardo's myth has steadily grown and acquired new luster. During the last four centuries, many of his scattered notebooks and lost codices have been reassembled, and they reveal Leonardo the scientist to be as astonishing as Leonardo the artist. His writings and drawings on anatomy, botany, mechanics, optics, flight, and military engineering prefigure inventions and discoveries made only in the present century.

Our post-Renaissance world marvels that a single individual could encompass so fully the seemingly opposed realms of spirit and matter. In futile attempts to explain the man and his genius, historians and psychiatrists have offered complex theories based on his

*This essay first appeared in the* East West Journal, *in July, 1980, and has been enlarged slightly for this book. The author, who was editor of* EWJ *at that time, would like to thank his colleagues, Sherman Goldman and Bill Tims, for their contributions to the original article. The sidebars appear for the first time.*

illegitimacy, possible homosexuality, left-handedness, misanthropy, and chronic failure to complete his works. But like the subject of his most famous work, the *Mona Lisa*, whose enchanting smile has beguiled every generation born into the modern world, the person behind the myth remains a puzzle.

Since Leonardo's time, Cartesian dualism has blocked our view of the world as a unification of mind and body. Like the Tower of Pisa, in the shadow of which it once flourished, the traditional art of visual diagnosis is widely dismissed today as a cultural eccentricity intended to reach some noble end but destined to fall from the accumulated weight of its own imbalance. However, the traditional science of physiognomy offers a panoramic viewpoint from which to understand the course of individual lives as well as the historical epochs in which they occur. By studying Leonardo's own face, we can understand the heaven-sent grace of which Vasari speaks and even penetrate the soul of the Renaissance itself—that cometlike Golden Age that briefly illuminated the Western world.

Leonardo, himself a lifelong student of visual diagnosis, would probably delight in this task. His writings on anatomy include plans for a book on "complexions, colors, and physiognomy." He compiled for his own reference a dictionary of heads, eyes, mouths, chins, necks, throats, shoulders, and noses. His careful study of the human form and exact drawings of torsos, tendons, intestines, and other anatomical features impressed upon him early in his career the importance of food and its effects on the human body. In an effort to understand "how nourishment proceeds to distribute itself through the veins," Leonardo pioneered the practice of medical dissection. In a Florentine hospital, he met an old man on his deathbed who explained that he had lived for one hundred years without sickness. After the man passed away, Leonardo examined the corpse to "ascertain the cause of so sweet a death" and found to his surprise that no animal fat covered the internal organs in the way he was used to seeing in cadavers. The conclusion was obvious and supported Leonardo's own abstention from animal food.

At the other end of the spectrum, Leonardo performed the first studies of the embryo and concluded, "As one mind governs two bodies inasmuch as the desires, the fears, and the pains of the mother are one with the pains, that is the bodily pains, and desires of the child which is in the body of the mother, in like manner the nourishment of the food serves for the child and it is nourished from the same cause as are the other parts of the mother . . . the mother desires a certain food and the child bears the mark of it."

# Leonardo's Embryological Constitution

any students of Leonardo's paintings are convinced that the body which he most often used as a model for his drawings was his own. In addition, several painters and sculptors of the period, including Michelangelo and Raphael, used Leonardo as a model in depicting famous figures of antiquity. We shall examine four of these likenesses for this physiognomic study. The first is Leonardo as the model for St. Michael from Botticini's *Tobias and the Three Archangels* begun in 1467 when Leonardo was fifteen. Second is the bronze statue of the young David sculpted by Verrocchio several years later when Leonardo, his brilliant young apprentice, would have been twenty-one. From middle age comes a pen-and-ink drawing showing the proportions of a man's head composed by Leonardo in front of a mirror when he was forty-four. The *Self-Portrait* in red chalk, dating to 1512, depicts Leonardo at age sixty.

Overall these three works present an appearance of incredible strength combined with noble refinement, a nearly perfect physique embodying great aspiration and will. Leonardo's bone structure is unusually angular, his cheekbones broad, his eyes deep-set in a square socket, his chin pronounced, his forehead large and craggy, and his hair curly. Yet none of these formidable constitutional features gives a feeling of harshness. Just as his structure seems about to reach sharpness, the play of the skin and bones bends off into a slight roundness. In the remarkably large yet round eyes we see softness, gentleness, and compassion over an even deeper level of energetic force. This inner spiral moving toward the center of the eyes shows intense determination and strength of character. Leonardo's resolve is also evident in the lower facial features. The mouth and nose almost curve up and in to meet one another in a compact way that expresses innate strength without tightness or rigidity. Leonardo's constitutional strength is further evidenced by the close and centered relationship of the facial features, strong bone structure, and extremely large, well-developed ears.

The oval structure of his head, the strong yet slightly downturned nose, the long eyebrows sloping down, and the perfect shape of the ears (straight, centered, flat against the head, wellrounded at the top, with detached, pendulous lobes) indicate that

13

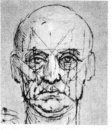

## Likenesses of Leonardo

*Top left, bronze statue of David by Verrocchio, Leonardo's teacher, 1471 (National Museum, Florence). Note Goliath's head at his feet. Top right, detail of St. Michael from* Tobias and the Three Archangels *attributed to Botticini, ca. 1467 (Uffizi Gallery, Florence). Lower right, Self-Portrait in red chalk, 1512 (Library, Turin). Lower left, sketch showing proportions of a man's face (ca. 1496 (Library, Turin).*

his mother ate predominantly vegetable-quality food during pregnancy. Whole grains in particular formed the staple of her meals, as can be seen in the oval, grainlike shape of St. Michael's and David's nostrils, in contrast to the more rounded nostrils of individuals whose mothers consumed meat or the elongated nostrils typically produced by a more tropical vegetarian diet high in fruit and raw foods.

In Leonardo's case, we know only that his mother, Caterina, was a young farm girl who conceived her son out of wedlock with Ser Piero, who was from a prosperous family of Florentine notaries or lawyers. Shortly thereafter, she left her son with the father's household in Vinci, a little town twenty miles from Florence. She eventually married a local farmer and virtually disappeared from her son's private and public life. Nevertheless, this largely anonymous peasant woman exercised the dominant effect of the two parents in the constitutional strengths and talents she bequeathed her child. This influence is clearly revealed in the right side of Leonardo's face whose features are more contracted than those of the left half. Produced by the earth's rotation on its axis from east to west, a spiral of centrifugal energy flows upwards on the right side of the body corresponding to the mother's influence. This expansive rising energy is called earth's force or yin energy in Oriental medical and philosophy. Complementary to this force is a stream of energy from the solar system and galaxy flowing downwards in a counterclockwise spiral to the left side and identified with the father. This contracting, gathering energy is called heaven's force or yang energy. One side of an individual's face is always a little more contracted (i.e., more compact, more yang, and therefore stronger) than the other. The heritage of Leonardo's mother, rooted in the soil of Tuscany and its native grains, contributed to Leonardo's sensitivity to the natural world and his tendency toward a soft, yin artistic expression in his work.

Though less pronounced, the influence of Leonardo's father is still quite strong, especially in the constitutional makeup of the nervous system. In the power of the forehead, the strength of the nose, and the full development of the eyebrows, we immediately perceive an individual of immense intellectual ability and breadth of thought. His father married several times and produced nine sons and two daughters before dying in 1504 at the age of eighty.

On the father's side, a close relationship between Leonardo and his grandfather (shown most clearly in the young David) is indicated by the contracted, unusually well-formed outer corner of the left

15

eye. Just as father and mother correspond with left and right sides, the respective halves of the face can be further divided to diagnose the influence of each grandparent. The inner corners of the eyes represent the grandmothers, the outer the grandfathers. In confirmation of this biological truth, we know that Leonardo's paternal grandfather lovingly recorded his grandson's christening and lived with and helped bring up the young prodigy while his father conducted business in Florence.

Young Leonardo's rearbrain (as seen in the strong crown of his head in the drawings and sculpture) is particularly well developed, indicating that the youth possessed a deep sense of the past and his "heaven-sent" origins. While the rearbrain serves the function of memory, the forebrain governs the capacity to dream, plan, and create the future. Overall, in Leonardo's physiognomy as in his works of art, we sense a masterful feel for the realm of yin: the feminine, the dark, the subtle, the musical, the passive, the receding; the world of plants and the kingdom of nature; the ebb and flow of water, vibrational sound, and the world of spirit. Yet all of these manifestations are held together masterfully with a yang center of strength, power, and clarity.

## Leonardo's Changing Condition

rom all accounts, Leonardo ate primarily grains and vegetables throughout his life. The family estate produced wheat and buckwheat. Growing up on the latter, the strongest of the staple cereal plants, would help explain Leonardo's vitality, endurance, and strength. Scribbled shopping lists found in his papers indicate purchases of millet, bread, maize, bran, kidney beans, broad beans, peas, panic grass, mushrooms, fruit, and wine. He was especially fond of pasta and minestrone soup. Except possibly for eggs, after age thirty when he is believed to have become completely vegetarian, Leonardo never ate animal products (not meat nor dairy food nor honey.) "The life of man is formed from things he eats," Leonardo wrote in his notebooks. "If you would keep healthy, follow this regimen: do not eat unless you feel inclined, and sup lightly: chew well and let what you take be well cooked and simple."

As an adult, Leonardo's staple grain seems to have been millet.

The small, yellow cereal is mentioned more often than any other in his notebooks both as a food and the incidental material of his experiments. Millet grains figure in his research on gravity, perspective, mechanics, and hydrodynamics. A renowned designer of costumes and clothes for courtly occasions, Leonardo advised using two kinds of millet as a filler for one fabric design. From these frequent allusions, we can deduce that the painter kept a regular supply of millet on hand, and when he wasn't having it for supper used its small grains to measure the mathematical properties of the flow of water or the force of gravity. Barley is also mentioned, once in a reminder to send "ears of [barley]corn to Florence" and again that "corn tossed up with a sieve leaps up in the form of a pyramid"—an observation some modern shoppers at a natural foods store may have made while weighing out grain in bulk. Leonardo also regularly consumed rice which had been introduced into northern Italy following the Crusades.

In Leonardo's paintings, we sense the effects of millet, brown rice, and other whole grains in the peace and inner strength of the main figures; the predominant grain-colored tones of gold, light brown, and yellow; a fascination with spiral shapes and motions; a clarity of perspective and the general orderliness and harmony of composition. Leonardo's most respected quality was patience, and he liked to say that " a strength of a painter is in his solitude." Physiologically, patience requires a healthy liver. Unlike millet, barley, and rice which are consumed in whole form and which tonify the liver, milled wheat including flour and pasta can overtax the liver, leading to irritability and anger. Of the five basic tastes, millet falls in the range of sweetness, the quality which we immediately associate with the faces and features of most of Leonardo's human figures.

The gentle tone to his work is further developed by his consumption of fruit. In his essays on art, he says he prefers to paint figures displaying "sweet fleshiness with simple folds and roundness of the limbs." The deep-red, blue, and wine-colored hues which complement Leonardo's golds, browns, and yellows further suggest the influence of fruit in his menu, as do the primeval landscapes in his paintings reminiscent of a geological period prior to the evolution of cereal grasses. Finally, the kinetic gestures of Leonardo's secondary figures reveal a predilection for grapes, strawberries, and melons. Note the intensity with which each disciple in *The Last Supper* is pointing, grasping, or moving. Such eagerness is a characteristic today of joggers, yogis, and others who drink large

*Detail showing Jesus and disciples from* **The Last Supper,** *1495 (Convent of Santa Maria delle Grazie, Milan). Note St. Thomas' upraised index finger.*

amounts of juice.

Taken in season, grown locally, cooked, and eaten in small amounts, fruit is an important and healthy part of a natural diet. However, taken out of season, imported across climatic zones, or eaten raw or in large amounts, fruit can be harmful to health, especially to the kidneys. On the face, kidney problems show up as darkness, puffiness, bulges, and, ultimately, circles and deep bags under the eyes—a progression easy to trace in the likenesses of Leonardo from youth through the prime of life to old age. Psychologically, kidney stagnation translates as fear, lack of stamina and will, sexual difficulties or ambivalence, and suspicion of others. Leonardo's lifelong kidney troubles help explain his fascination with death, violence, and instruments of war; his expressed distaste for sexuality and lack of family life; and his brooding mistrust of others and "fruity" tendency to be "ripped off" by patrons and associates. In the history of world art, Leonardo's paintings are the most stolen and vandalized;

they have been attacked with stones, knives, and once even a revolver. This karma would appear to be partly a legacy of this biological tendency.

Excess oil in cooking also appears to have aggravated Leonardo's kidney condition. As he grew older, the area between the eyes—corresponding to the gall bladder—gradually expanded, indicating stagnation and overproduction of bile. After age fifty, Leonardo wore spectacles, poor eyesight being linked to troubles in the liver and gall bladder. Emotionally, an oily condition in the body contributes to isolation, creates a barrier between the individual and the environment, and, in extreme instances, leads to reclusiveness. In his notes, Leonardo mentions a home remedy for gallstones, indicating he may have been aware of this condition.

Excess water may also have contributed to his weak kidney condition. As the years progressed, Leonardo's drawings, paintings, and notebooks portray an increasing obsession with water. He sketched swirling waters, rivers overflowing their banks, floods and deluges, and great torrents inundating the plains and their inhabitants. Physiologically, these point to overworked kidneys and bladder. Leonardo's curiosity about natural order led him to study the formation of mountains, rivers, and rocks. On one climb, he found fossilized seaweed and shells in sedimentary mountains that indicated the earth was once covered with oceans. Seaweed, which is rich in minerals, would have helped strengthen this condition, but seaweed was not part of the usual diet in Renaissance Italy.

In spite of developing health problems, Leonardo stayed in peak shape over the years. He refrained from violence and abhorred cruelty to animals (paying merchants to release caged songbirds), yet he possessed great physical strength and reputedly could bend a horseshoe with his bare hands. Mentally, Leonardo amazed his contemporaries with his powers of endurance. During the painting of *The Last Supper*, he worked for long periods without food or drink.

As for doctors, Leonardo warned, "Strive to preserve your health; and in this you will the better succeed in proportion as you keep clear of the physicians." Undoubtedly he followed his own advice. Nevertheless, as the portraits show, Leonardo's internal organs gradually weakened over the years. In addition to kidney and gall bladder trouble, we see in his *Self Portrait* of 1512 distension in the intestines as indicated by the bulging lower lip, drawn cheeks, and horizontal lines on the forehead. Seven years later, after an illness of several months, he died. According to Vasari, his passing, in the arms of the king of France, his last patron, was a sweet one.

# Mona Lisa

ualities of the heart as well as the eye influence a painter's hand. In his treatise on painting, Leonardo advised young artists, "Look about you and take the best parts of many beautiful faces, of which the beauty is confirmed rather by public fame than by your own judgment; for you might be mistaken and choose faces which have some resemblance to your own. For it would seem that such resemblances often please us; and if you should be ugly, you would select faces that were not beautiful and you would then make ugly faces, as many painters do. For often a master's shapes resemble himself."

The identity of Mona Lisa, as well as the source of the painting's almost irresistible attraction for nearly everyone who sees it, is one of the great mysteries of art. According to Vasari, Leonardo received a commission in 1503 from Francesco del Giocondo, a leading citizen of Florence, to paint a portrait of his beautiful young wife. "This figure of Leonardo's has such a pleasant smile," the biographer states, "that it seemed rather divine than human, and was considered marvelous, an exact copy of life."

Historians have subsequently discovered other references to the painting which cast doubt on this account. Today there are as many candidates for Mona Lisa as the mysterious Dark Lady of the Shakespearean Sonnets. The favorites of the scholarly world include Isabelle d'Este, Leonardo's patroness from Mantua; Costanza d'Avalos, the Duchess of Francaville; various Florentine courtesans; a personification of the Virgin Mary, Eve, or the eternal feminine; or even a male figure such as Leonardo's pupils Francesca del Melza and Salai. Whomever the likeness represents, the portrait was never formally completed and presented to the Giocondos or any other benefactor as was customary. Rather Leonardo chose to keep the *Mona Lisa* for himself and on rare occasions displayed it in his quarters. Despite this limited exposure, the *Mona Lisa* immediately revolutionalized portraiture, and its style and technique were widely imitated. Following Leonardo's death, Francis I, King of France, the artist's last patron, displayed his work at his chateau in Fontainebleau. The *Mona Lisa* has been the prize treasure of the French government ever since.

The *Mona Lisa* conveys three immediate impressions: in the face, neck, and hands we see pleasantness, in the eyes and smile we perceive secrecy, in the landscape we feel loneliness. Constitutionally, Mona Lisa impresses us with her strong, high forehead; bony eye sockets and angular cheek bones; a long nose, pointed at the tip and dipping slightly down; and pronounced chin. These solid, yang features show profound inner strength, a fully developed nervous system, and a superior intellect. The strong influence of heaven's force through the father is softened externally by the round cast to the facial features, the suppleness of the skin, the warmth and luster of the eyes, and the unusual length of the fingers.

**Mona Lisa, *1503 (Louvre, Paris). Note contraction on the right (mother's) side.***

If we hold a piece of paper vertically bisecting Mona Lisa's face, we see that the right side is tighter or more contracted, indicating the dominant influence of the mother and a practical outlook on life. In the eyes also, the firm outer angle to the left corner shows the relatively important influence of the paternal grandfather in the subject's life. Although we cannot see the ears, these other constitutional features together reveal that Mona Lisa came from a family with strong agricultural roots and a cereal-based diet. In childhood, youth, and early adulthood, Mona Lisa continued to eat primarily grains and vegetables. We see this in her remarkable poise and centeredness, the clarity and penetration of the eyes, and the absence of those facial lines, discolorations, and swellings normally produced by regular consumption of meat and/or dairy products.

Nevertheless, the tightness about the mouth indicates slightly contracted intestines. Mona Lisa's hands are large and puffy, disproportionate to her fingers, signifying congestion. The puffiness under her eyes, caused by excess water retained in the urinary system, warns of developing kidney troubles.

By studying her underlying physiognomy in this way, we can

# Nine Star Ki:
# Leonardo's Character

Nine Star Ki, the system of astrology and directionology underlying the I Ching, the Aztec Calendar, and other ancient cosmologies, divides people into nine star types: flexible One Waters, gentle Two Soils, romantic Three Trees, idealistic Four Trees, balanced Five Soils, disciplined Six Metals, social Seven Metals, visionary Eight Soils, and passionate Nine Fires.

Leonardo was born in an Eight Soil year and like many natives of this house was serious, silent, intelligent, and very refined. By nature, Eight Soils are bright and optimistic, hardworking, and quiet and introspective. However, their self-reliance often causes them to become isolated and may be viewed by others as stubbornness. They are wary of relationships, but establish lasting friendships once a bond is made. Their success usually comes later in life, often through the support of seniors or inheritance from their father or grandfather. Their minds are very orderly, they have a keen sense of justice, and they make excellent planners, scientists, and educators. At an energetic level, Eight Soil corresponds to the period between midnight and dawn—or late winter and early spring—and many of the great revolutionary thinkers of humanity have been born under this sign. In addition to Leonardo—who spanned the medieval and modern worlds and embodies the transition from cultural darkness to light—Eight Soils historically have included Descartes, Mao Zedong, and George Ohsawa. Like many Eight Soils who rebel against authority inwardly, Leonardo expressed his opposition to the excesses of the Medieval Church by refusing to paint haloes around his figures and portraying gathering tempests and deluges in the background of his paintings. He also held back his discoveries of fossils that called into question the Biblical account of creation.

In the Oriental Zodiac, Leonardo was born in a Monkey year. Monkey types have very active, creative minds and enjoy a well developed sense of humor, have clever personalities, and like to entertain others. Today we honor Leonardo as a painter and scientific forerunner. However, in his own time, he was

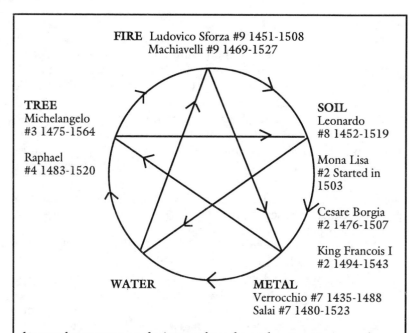

**FIRE** Ludovico Sforza #9 1451-1508
Machiavelli #9 1469-1527

**TREE**
Michelangelo
#3 1475-1564

Raphael
#4 1483-1520

**SOIL**
Leonardo
#8 1452-1519

Mona Lisa
#2 Started in
1503

Cesare Borgia
#2 1476-1507

King Francois I
#2 1494-1543

**WATER**

**METAL**
Verrocchio #7 1435-1488
Salai #7 1480-1523

known by many as a designer of masks and costumes, a producer of carnivals and balls, and as a master illusionist. He created marvelous entertainments for his wealthy patrons and their courts, designing fantastic sets, mechanical devices, and other diversions for religious festivals, holidays, and weddings. One of his most famous creations was the Masque of the Planets, dramatizing the order of the infinite universe.

In Florence, he joined the Company of the Caldron, a group of artists who held noisy feasts in which they composed pictures not with brushes and oils but with food. Outrageous and grotesque compositions were made with lasagne, sausage, jelly, cheese, and other goods. Though a vegetarian, Leonardo participated good-naturedly in these revels. In his quarters, he kept a menagerie of birds and animals. In a famous letter, Andrea Corsali, a traveler returning from the East, observed that the Hindus respected the life of all creatures, even insects, "like our Leonardo da Vinci."

In his love of jokes and riddles, festivals and fireworks, Leonardo's monkey character shines forth. In the all-knowing smile of Mona Lisa, the impish smile of John the Baptist, and other enigmatic expressions on his canvases, we also see a hint of Leonardo's underlying character. ❖

solve the puzzle of Mona Lisa's identity. The canvas depicts Leonardo himself! We see the same eyes, same nose, same lips, same chin, same constitution, same condition, same mother, same father, same grandparents, same diet, same dream. From the bone structure of the head to the corners of the eyes, from the strength of the right side of the face to the bulge under the eyes, we are confronted with a likeness of the painter himself. The female form in which Leonardo chose to compose his ultimate self-portrait would naturally appeal to an inventive and creative mind which delighted in riddles, musical rebuses, word play, and handwriting that went backwards from right to left. Just as we must hold Leonardo's notebooks up to a mirror to read their script, he summons us to pass through the looking glass of sexual complementarity to recognize the true features and spirit of his greatest painting.

Mona Lisa appears to be about thirty, or ten years older than young David to which, nonetheless, her face bears striking resemblance. While we do not know the exact circumstances surrounding the painting's composition, the general background is readily accessible. In 1500 Leonardo returned to live in Florence for the first time in eighteen years. When he left his native capital in 1482 at age thirty, he embarked upon a professional career (originally as a musician) under the patronage of Ludovico Sforza (Il Moro), the Duke of Milan. Leonardo's happy and carefree days in Florence, first at Verrocchio's workshop and later as an independent member of the artists' guild, came to an end. The illustrious young man soon found himself the pawn of rulers and bishops whose devotion to music and art was primarily mercenary. For nearly twenty years, he labored in the vineyards of courtly patronage.

Returning home to Florence after so long must have lifted his spirits, but Cesare Borgia, the ambitious commander in Romagna, summoned Leonardo to be his architect and chief military engineer. An offer made by the ruthless and cruel Borgia, shortly to be immortalized as Machiavelli's *The Prince*, could not be refused. Accompanied by Machiavelli, Leonardo joined Borgia's encampment at Piombino in the summer of 1502 and lent his inventive talents to the prince's nefarious schemes. The engineering project which occupied most of Leonardo's time involved devising plans to divert the course of the Arno River to deprive Pisa of its water and make Florence directly accessible by sea. He also pursued studies in the construction of a gigantic crossbow, rapid-fire artillery, and other weapons of mass destruction which he had begun earlier during his service in Milan.

*Leonardo's drawing of assault vehicles (British Museum, London). The script is written from left to right in a mirrorlike hand.*

After Borgia's victory in 1503, culminating in the infamous murder of his own commanders, Leonardo returned to Florence and began the preliminary drawing for *The Battle of Anghiari,* the sweeping mural of men and horses at war which reminds us today of the theme and mood depicted in Picasso's *Guernica,* the stark masterpiece that has become an icon of 20th century art in the way that *Mona Lisa* symbolized the Renaissance. It is noteworthy to study the physiognomy of the men in Leonardo's battle scenes and the aptly named *Grotesque Heads,* for they clearly display signs of heavy meat, dairy, and sugar consumption unlike the visages of his religious portraits. Against this backdrop of intrigue, violence, and bloodshed, Leonardo began the *Mona Lisa* in late 1503 or 1504.

Pictorially, the canvas is the tribute of a cynical man of middle age to the innocence and promise of youth. The *Mona Lisa* is the portrait of a soul which has sold itself to the highest bidder and is now penitent. We do not know what dreams young Leonardo entertained when he first left Florence, but a young man's ambitions in Renaissance Italy easily turned to politics. Despots like Sforza (on whose uncompleted equestrian statue Leonardo spent sixteen years) and Borgia could prevail only because their subjects, counselors, and performing artists shared the same emerging mercantile doctrine that "the end justifies the means." During Leonardo's lifetime, assassination became an accepted political tool and the Inquisition reached its height. Just five years before the *Mona Lisa* was started, the reformer Savonarola was burned for heresy in Florence's main square. Once the cloak of obedience was donned, it was hard to take off for conscience' sake. Leonardo, the crown jewel in so many princely caps, could not write about such misgivings, even backwards in a mirrorlike script. Instead, his later paintings became the vehicle through which he expressed his social conscience. "The good painter must paint . . . man and the ideas in man's mind," he declared in his treatise advising young artists.

In the *Mona Lisa*, the artist, now fifty, looks back on himself at thirty. On the canvas, he expresses all of the locked up energies of the intervening years, hints at the obstacles that have blocked his way, and laughs sweetly at the seductions and favors lavished upon him. Yet the result is so subtly accomplished that Mona Lisa appears to reveal nothing. The theories and suspicions of the art critics, thrown off by the female form and the quest for the historical Mona Lisa, glance harmlessly aside. Her secret smile remains intact. Her health and vitality—rarely seen in the modern world—dazzle and mystify us.

The French come closest to unmasking her identity and affectionately refer to her as "La Courtesan." But Mona Lisa is not a streetwalker in the usual sense. She is the farmer's daughter (Renaissance Gothic style) about to leave the land and its simple virtues for the glamor and easy pleasures of the city. In middle age she will become prosperous Florence herself, the prototype of the modern city-state whose first family, the Medicis, financed both sides of the Hundred Years' War, controlled popes and kings, built a many-sided commercial empire with branches in every European capital, and compounded their capital and interest from the blood and tears of a peasantry uprooted by the new commodity economy. She is traditional humanity on the threshold of the Industrial Revolution.

Mona Lisa is pregnant with the modern world. She contains in her fertile brow (which, of course, is Leonardo's) the seeds of nearly all the major inventions and discoveries of the next five centuries. Each one of us is her step-child, inhabitants of an alienated landscape in which hearts are bought and sold and all have their price. The terrain behind Mona Lisa frames the bleak and barren future which Leonardo sensed approaching. Like the Arno River which he sought to divert, he foresees the artificial course of human history that lies ahead and a reverse in the flow of culture and civilization. In a composition known as the *Deluge of Objects*, dated to 1498, Leonardo drew a rain of implements, including tools, instruments, and other mechanical devices. Commenting on humanity's materialism, he wrote on the ground below: "Oh human misery: of how many things you make yourself the slave for money!"

During most of his adult life, Leonardo devoted his heaven-sent energies to commemorating various rulers' colossal egos in bronze and stone. Now, at last, back in Florence, the city of his youth, he had the opportunity (or perhaps seized it when a portrait was commissioned) to express the innermost depths of his soul. The painting may have started out as the likeness of a young bride or "the best part of many beautiful faces," but in the end he fell victim to his own prophecy, "for often a master's shapes resemble himself." For the next sixteen years, until the day he died, Leonardo kept the *Mona Lisa* by his side, first in Florence, then Milan, Rome, and finally Amboise in France where he spent his last days. Her irresistible beauty—the light of his own soul—was for sale, but who could afford her if not himself? The caged songbird was finally set free to realize its dream of flight.

**Deluge of Objects,** *ca. 1498 (Royal Library, Windsor).*

# The Renaissance

enaissance means rebirth. The word was first used by Vasari in *The Lives of the Painters* to describe the brilliant rejuvenation of art and learning that flourished in Florence in the fourteenth and fifteenth centuries. Not since the Golden Age of Athens in the fifth century B.C. has the culture of a single city made such an imprint upon the Western imagination. The Modern Age still recognizes the Renaissance as the most magnificent flower of Occidental civilization.

From today's perspective, the spirit of the Renaissance was very close to that of China. In outlook both cultures acknowledged the primacy of heaven and earth, yet were essentially humanistic. In questions of ethics, both laid stress on everyday life and practical wisdom and relied for nourishment on the classics. In science, both emphasized direct observation and technical inventiveness. In art, both excelled at landscapes and portraits detailing the flora and fauna of the natural world and strived to achieve precision of detail and immediacy in impact.

In his classic *Science and Civilization in China*, Joseph Needham traces the transmission from East to West of nearly all of the technical discoveries and inventions from antiquity until the start of the Industrial Revolution. From China came the wheelbarrow, the sailing-carriage, the wagon-mill, harnesses for drought animals, the crossbow, the kite, the technique of deep-drilling, the mastery of cast iron, the suspension bridge, canal lock-gates, the square-pallet chain pump, the edge-runner mill, metallurgical blowing-engines, the rotary fan and winnowing machine, the piston-bellows, the horizontal warp-loom and the drawloom, numerous navigational inventions including the fore-and-aft rig and the stern-post rudder, gunpowder, the magnetic compass, paper, printing and movable type, and porcelain. Only four major mechanical techniques moved in the other direction from West to East: the screw, the force-pump for liquids, the crankshaft, and clockwork.

In the late Middle Ages the transmission of technology from the East declined as the Mongols overran China and the illustrious Sung Dynasty came to an end. But in Italy, the continuity of scientific progress continued as several generations of brilliant thinkers, of whom Leonardo was foremost, set in motion the gears and wheels of the modern world. In addition to drawings for manned flight, submarines, the bicycle and modern weaponry, Leonardo sketched twenty of the twenty-two principal components of modern machinery including the lever, cam, pulley, and flywheel. In the breadth of his interests and depths of his skill, he distilled within one lifetime a scientific output roughly equal to that of China over thirty or forty centuries and anticipated the developments of the next five centuries.

Leonardo's innovations in painting rival his contributions to mechanics and, like the latter, display peculiarly Oriental influences. Roy McMullen writes in *Mona Lisa: The Picture and the Myth* (Houghton Mifflin, 1975),

> [Although Leonardo] most certainly never saw a Sung or Ming painting, his somewhat Chinese feeling for distant mountains, for landscape as both a fact and a symbol, and for the wideness of the world led him in the *Mona Lisa* to reject converging lines and adopt a strikingly Chinese combination of aerial perspective with shifting viewpoints and parallel bands of scenery. His *sfumato* [shading] is comparable to the tonal technique of Chinese ink painting, his wall-stain notion is remindful of Zen blots, and his idea of the microcosm and the macrocosm, although thoroughly Western, is in exact agreement with part of the old Chinese outlook.

Did Leonardo visit the Far East? Some historians believe he did and speculate about gaps in the chronology of his life. His notebooks describe a visit to the Near East. His personal library included the fictional travels to China of John de Mandeville, as well as volumes on chiromancy, dragons and other imaginary animals, and Arab treatises on health. Shortly before starting the *Mona Lisa*, in the service of Borgia, Leonardo designed plans for a colossal bridge to span East and West at the request of the Sultan of Constantinople. In Vinci, Leonardo's uncle, Francesco, raised silkworms on the family estate. Over the years, the artist's religious themes gave way to more secular subjects, and some of them contain what is believed to be his cryptographic signature in the form of a spiral design reminiscent of Islamic calligraphy. The neckline to Mona Lisa's dress, for example, contains a looping, knotlike pattern that evidently puns on the words *vincire* (to knot, to fetter, to lace) and *Vinci*.

Like Easterners, Leonardo also viewed the earth as an image of humans. "The earth," he wrote, "has a vegetative life; its flesh is the

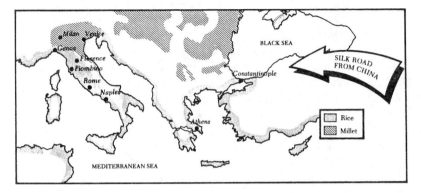

*Map depicting rice and millet farming in Southern Europe, A.D. 1500.*
*Source:* **Times Atlas of World History.**

oil, its bones the disposition and assembly of rocks that form the mountains; its cartilage is limestone, its blood the living streams." Similarly, the body was a microcosm of the world as a whole. "The cosmography of the *mondo minor* [microcosm] will be revealed to you in twelve entire figures," he observed, "in the same order as Ptolemy followed in his cosmography. Thus I shall divide the limbs as he divides the earth into provinces; then I shall speak of the functions of each part of the body in its own place, putting before your eyes a representation of the whole form and substance of a man, and every local movement by means of its parts." This quest and his search for correspondences, such as "the lung of the earth," echo the basic teachings of the *Yellow Emperor's Classic.* The textbook of Oriental medicine and philosophy, dating back thousands of years, draws a parallel between the twelve principal meridians of the body and the rivers of the earth, as well as the other organs, systems, and functions and topographical features.

Whether or not Leonardo actually travelled to the Levant, Marco Polo's description of Cathay still exercised a powerful hold over the Renaissance imagination in the nearly two centuries since it had been composed. By the fifteenth century, following the eastward march of the Crusades and the westward advance of the Mongols, the Italian city-states controlled the western termini of the Silk Road from China. Venetian and Genoese ships ruled the Mediterranean and carried the fabulous cargoes of silks, spices, cottons, and drugs to their final destinations in England, Flanders, and the German states. (Mona Lisa's own dress, mantle, and veil appear to be made of imported Chinese silk.) At the center of this commercial network

# Nine Star Ki:
# The Age of Adventure

Personal life is influenced primarily by the yearly and monthly Nine Star Ki cycles. The life of society mirrors larger spirals, including an 81-year-cycle that gives a unique character and energy to a period lasting several generations. The Renaissance era in which Leonardo da Vinci lived was governed by Six White Metal energy, during which society reflects the hard, gathering tendency of metal nature.

| 5 | 1 | 3 |
|---|---|---|
| 4 | 6 | 8 |
| 9 | 2 | 7 |

1469-1550

The age was dominated by inwardly directed, self-disciplined leaders who had a strong sense of direction and purpose. The years from 1469 to 1550 were the age of adventure, the age of discovery and exploration, the age of the great painters and sculptors. It was the era of the rise of the individual: the development of perspective in art, the spread of printing which made books, especially the Bible, available to the average person, and the Reformation, which enshrined individual conscience.

During this era, Five Soil governing overall social balance and imbalance was situated in the house of Four Tree, indicating that war, disease (e.g., the plague), and other forms of conflict were on the rise.

Metallic talismans of the age included the nails which Luther used to affix his theses to the church door in Wittenberg, the founding of the Sikh religion (whose adherents carry small knives), and the introduction of forks and pocket watches.    ❖

lay Florence, the banking capital of Renaissance Europe. Florence's first family, the Medici, spun such an intricate web of connections that they seemed to complement the nearly invisible silkworms spinning their cocoons at the other end of the trade line.

Columbus's discovery of the Americas, Vasco da Gama's journey around Africa, and the explorations of Amerigo Vespucci at the turn of the sixteenth century marked the end of the old overland

# Diagnosis:
# Leonardo's Unfinished Work

*Detail from Raphael's* **Plato** *(using Leonardo as a model)*

According to a famous story, Leonardo and Michelangelo first met by accident in a Florentine plaza. The young sculptor taunted the old master for not completing the bronze horse that he had labored on for many years and implied that his day was over. A Three Tree, Michelangelo's energy—rapid, strong, and explosive—was counter to Leonardo's—slow, gentle, deliberate.

Though cruelly spoken, the jibe was true. Leonardo left almost all of his works, from the great horse to his artistic masterpieces, incomplete. These included *The Battle of Anghiari, The Virgin with Saint Anne, The Last Supper, The Mona Lisa, The Adoration of the Magi, St. Jerome,* and others.

Vasari, the great art historian, attributed this to Leonardo being "capricious and unstable." "His intelligence of art made him take on many projects but never finish any of them, since it seemed to him that the hand would never achieve the requisite perfection." Leonardo's inability to finish his work constitutes one of the great mysteries surrounding his life and career, and art critics and psychoanalysts have developed a lucrative industry speculating on its cause.

From the view of Oriental medicine and philosophy, there is a simple biological explanation for this tendency. The intestines govern our basic vitality and weakness in the intestines can lead to indecision, frequent interruptions and delays, or lack of "guts" or stamina to complete a project. The Freudian view that our bowel movements unconsciously influence our thoughts and behavior contains a lot of truth.

In Leonardo's case, while blessed with a strong constitution and eating a basically well centered grain-based diet, the great artist enjoyed eating too many fruits, sweets, and other more yin fare. Over time, this led to digestive troubles, especially expanded intestines and chronic constipation—the inability to form regular bowel movements because of a lack of contractive power and thus the inability to see things to completion. The large intestine governs these functions, and in Oriental medicine the large intestine meridian begins in the first finger of the hand.

*Leonardo's* **St. John the Baptist,** *ca. 1515 (Louvre, Paris).*

Pains, aches, unusual motion, or other abnormal problems or movements associated with this finger are a sign of developing weakness of the intestines.

Leonardo's paintings frequently highlight this finger—and hence—meridian. *John the Baptist* has his right index finger upraised. *Bacchus'* index finger similarly is emphasized, as are fingers in *The Adoration of the Magi* and *The Last Supper*. (Pointing upward is a more yin gesture, while pointing downward is more yang.) In fact, the upraised index finger became such a trademark signature of Leonardo that Raphael in his famous portrait of Plato—believed to be based on a likeness of Leonardo as an old man with a flowing beard—shows him with an index finger raised.

To the churchman of the day and to generations of art critics, this sign has been taken as a pious gesture to God and the heavens above. Physiologically, it also points inwardly to Leonardo's own intestinal weakness. The reason for many of our difficulties, like Leonardo's inability to complete his masterpieces, is usually very simple, obvious, and close at hand. The order of the infinite universe which the great master sought to mirror in his works is marvelous indeed! ❖

caravans and the Italian mercantile system. The economy of the Renaissance, built upon the wealth of Asia, collapsed and the commercial center of power gravitated to Spain, Portugal, France, and England. Silk for men's and women's apparel henceforth arrived from China in frigates sailing around Africa.

The Chinese fabrics and fragrances form the petals of the Renaissance flower, but for its roots we must look, as in an actual plant, to the soil. The seeds of that brilliance are the seeds of Oriental civilization itself: rice and millet. By Leonardo's time, the two grains that had nourished Chinese culture for millennia entered southern Europe and were cultivated along the entire rim of the Mediterranean coast. Florence at this time occupied the geographical center of rice cultivation in the West (*see map on p. 30*). During the Renaissance, millet grew in the area encompassing Milan and Venice.

About the time of Leonardo's death, maize from the New World entered Europe and because of its higher yields quickly replaced millet and rice. Northern Italy's two-hundred-year experiment with the whole grains of the Far East—and thereby the Renaissance— came to an abrupt end. The most striking features of the Renaissance are the amazing power of its brilliance and equally amazing suddenness with which that brilliance faded. Its overall impression is that of a gorgeous and swiftly fading flower.

Why did the flower blossom so briefly? From the time of the Indo-Europeans through ancient Rome and the medieval Crusades, the West embarked on a course leading to universal destruction. Excessive amounts of meat, poultry, eggs, salt, bread, and baked food fueled this march toward Armageddon. The only thing the West lacked was a means, a vertical overview or strategy, to carry out is horizontal mission. The curious and inventive mind produced by whole grains was instrumental to planting the seed of modern science in the garden of those who would ultimately let it grow out of control. The materialism of the last five centuries is now on the wane, and when it reaches the limit of its development—probably in the early 21st century—a new world devoted to more humanistic values will be born. In the present cycle, technological advance is the means by which the old order will reach its peak, destroy itself, and prepare the soil for a new cycle. Thus during the Renaissance, as the technological culmination of a long transmission stretching back to antiquity, the East cross-pollinated the West with its grains in a curious fulfillment of the order of nature.

By the generation following Leonardo's lifetime, the temperate seeds that the Renaissance humanists broadcast had been over-

*Postscript:*
# Computer Science
# Meets Oriental Diagnosis

Seven years after this article appeared in *East West Journal*, Lillian Schwartz, a researcher at Bell Laboratories, demonstrated on the basis of modern computer analysis that Leonardo used his own features for the composition of the *Mona Lisa*. Matching the the faces of Leonardo's *Self-Portrait* in red chalk and the *Mona Lisa*, she concluded in the lead article in the January, 1987, issue of *Art & Antiquities* magazine that they were identical. "The images were set to the same scale by making the distances between the centers of the eye pupils equal to each other," Schwartz explained. "The self-portrait was then flopped left to right in order to match the pose of the *Mona Lisa*. Both pictures were bisected along vertical lines centered on the tips of the nose and the halves then aligned using the nose tips. Juxtaposing the images was all that was needed to fuse them: the relative locations of the nose, mouth, chin, eyes, and forehead in one precisely matched the other. Merely flipping up the corner of the mouth would produce the mysterious smile, and a reduction of the pouch under Leonardo's eye is all that is necessary to match the Mona Lisa's horizontal lid." "[T]he sphinxlike riddle posed by the *Mona Lisa's* smile has been solved," Schwartz concluded. "Artist and model were one and the same. The *Mona Lisa* is Leonardo da Vinci's portrait of himself." ❖

grown by extreme tropical varieties. Potatoes, tomatoes, sugarcane, and other tropical foodstuffs not suited to physical and mental vitality poured into Europe. In the seventeenth and eighteenth centuries, the West forgot its native grains and invented modern milling and food processing. Scholars questioned the very existence of heaven and traditional sciences like physiognomy and dietetics fell out of favor. Art lost its roots in the soil and sky. Under the influence of Cartesian dualism, spirit and matter went their separate ways, the specialists took over, and the technical means to annihilation were perfected. In this way, we can see Leonardo as both the father of the modern world and the architect of its demise. As a scientist, he betrayed an appalling callousness toward mass destruction. As an artist, he exhibited a limitless compassion and tenderness for life.

Today we are at the beginning of a new Renaissance. Rice, millet, and other whole grains have leapt the Atlantic and Pacific and are the dietary foundation for a new planetary culture and civilization. The organic natural foods movement, the holistic health revolution, and spreading environmental awareness are the pillars of strength, harmony, and balance that will result in the flourishing of the arts and sciences and the dawn of a new era for humanity. Macrobiotics—the way of health and peace—is the midwife of this biological and spiritual transformation.

The unifying spirit of Leonardo da Vinci has been lost, but his eyes still look out at us from the *Mona Lisa* and smile at our quandary. He foresees the centuries of inhumanity that lie ahead and knows that this spiral too must pass and give way to another based on the timeless humanistic values of his childhood and youth. "The water which you touch in a river," he once wrote, "is the last of that which has passed and the first of that which is to come. The same is true of the present moment: Life [*bios*] well spent is long [*macro*]." ❖

# Select Bibliography

Bramly, Serge, *Leonardo: Discovering the Life of Leonardo da Vinci*, Edward Burlingame Books, 1991.

Freud, Sigmund, *Leonardo da Vinci and a Memory of His Childhood*, 1910.

Heydenreich, Ludwig H., *Leonardo: The Last Supper*, Viking Press, 1974.

McMullen, Ray, *Mona Lisa: The Picture and the Myth*, Houghton-Mifflin, 1975.

Needham, Joseph, *Science and Civilization of China*, Cambridge University Press, 7 volumes, 1954-83.

Richter, Irma A., editor, *Selections from the Notebooks of Leonardo Da Vinci*, Oxford University Press, 1952.

Schwartz, Lillian, "Leonardo's Mona Lisa: Her Identity Revealed," *Art & Antiques*, January, 1987, pp. 50-55, 80.

Turner, A. Richard, *Inventing Leonardo*, Alfred A. Knopf, 1993.

Vasari, Giorgi, *Lives of the Artists*, Penguin, 1965.

# Christopher Columbus

*"There will come a time in later years*
*when Ocean shall loosen the bonds*
*by which we have been confined,*
*when an immense land shall be revealed*
*and Tiphys [pilot of the Argonauts] shall disclose new worlds,*
*and Thule [Iceland] will no longer be*
*the most remote of countries."*
—Seneca, Medea, 1st century A.D.

*"And in that day there shall be a root of Jesse which shall stand for an ensign of the people: to it shall the Gentiles seek; and his rest shall be glorious. And it shall come to pass in that day that the Lord shall set His hand again the second time to recover the remnant of His people which shall be left, from Assyria, and from Egypt . . . and from the islands of the sea."*
—Isaiah

*"I am not the first Admiral of my family—let them give me the name they will, for after all, David, a very wise King, kept ewes and later was made a King of Jerusalem, and I am the servant of that same Lord who raised David to that state."*
—Columbus, The Book of Prophecies

*"I have been very attentive and have tried very hard to find out if there is any gold here. I have seen a few natives who wear a little piece of gold hanging from a hole in their nose."*
—Columbus, Journal, October 13, 1492

*"In these unknown lands where Christopher Columbus has stepped, lives a people, naked, vegetarian, who believe in one God and ask but to be taught to believe in Jesus Christ. All these islands and territories, abounding in gold, spices and treasure, situated west and south of a line that runs from the North to the South Pole, a hundred leagues west of the Isles of the Azores and Cape Verde, are allocated to the Catholic Kings . . ."*
—Papal Bull, 1493

*"Zen is being able to see the North Star in the Southern sky."*
— The Book of Tea

---

*Overleaf: Woodcut based on oldest known portrait of Columbus commissioned by Paulus Jovius, published in 1575*

# Christopher Columbus
# Zen Navigator

 or nearly five hundred years, Columbus has been portrayed as an Italian, a devoted Christian, and a bearer of salvation to the Western Hemisphere. On the eve of the Second World War, Salvador de Madariaga, a Spanish diplomatic and literary critic, electrified the scholarly world by writing a biography in which he claimed that Columbus was the descendant of Spanish Jews, whose family had fled to Genoa to escape religious persecution. He theorized that although his conversion may have been genuine, Columbus lived a double life in which his secret Jewish identity played a pivotal role. Although dismissed in the wake of anti-Semitism during the war, Madariaga's thesis has won widespread support in the last generation. As Robert Fuson, a professor of geography at the University of South Florida, chairman of the First International Columbus Symposium, and consultant to the National Geographic Society's Columbus project, writes in his introduction to a new translation of Columbus' journal, "Salvador de Madariaga [and other researchers] have provided more than enough documentation to convince any objective person."

The name *Columbus* is a Latinized spelling of the family name that was used by his brother, Bartholomew, when he visited England on Christopher's behalf and sought the backing of King Henry VII. As such, it has been used by English-speaking writers since. In

*This essay is developed from material presented in health care lectures at the Kushi Institute in Becket in 1991 and 1992 during the five hundredth anniversary of Columbus' discovery of America.*

Spain, Columbus himself used the family name Colón, as did his son, his brother, and the King and Queen in their official documents. Today throughout the Caribbean, Latin America, and the Spanish-speaking world, Columbus is known as Cristobal Colón. Colón—and its Portuguese variant, Colom, which Columbus used in Portugal—is a common name among Jewish families, especially in Catalonia, the southeast region of Spain, and in Majorca, a Mediterranean island that was home to many Catalan-speaking Jews and Jewish cartographers. In the biography of his father, Ferdinand Colón says that his father "chose to leave in obscurity all that related to his birthplace and family" except to say that his name meant "dove." In Catalan, *Colom* is the word meaning dove. Columbus' letters and notebooks are written in Spanish with characteristic Catalanisms and the chief missionary and soldier to accompany him on his First Voyage were from Catalonia. In contrast, historians have been unable to find any writings in Columbus' hand in Italian, and none of his signatures are signed Colombo, the Italian version of his name. Seeking to learn the truth of his background, Ferdinand writes that he went to Genoa but could find no trace of the family.

According to Ferdinand, his father was born in 1447, four years earlier than the date later claimed by partisans of his Italian origin. In 1453, the Church ordered that all Jews on Majorca become Christian. Many families then—as later throughout Spain—converted to Christianity. (By the end of the 15th century, there were an estimated 300,000 Jewish converts in Spain.) Known as *conversos* or New Christians, some of these converts genuinely embraced their new religion. However, many secretly continued to practice the ways of their forefathers while outwardly appearing as model Catholics. In 1480, King Ferdinand and Queen Isabella authorized the Inquisition to root out false converts from Judaism. In the resulting witchhunt—including false accusations, torture, and execution—thousands of Jewish descent were severely punished and their property was confiscated. In the first eight years of the Inquisition, 700 persons were put to death. (Altogether the Inquisition claimed 341,000 victims, including 32,000 burned at the stake.) In Valencia, a city off the Majorcan coast where the persecution appears to have begun, four Coloms were burned to death as early as 1461. The Inquisition was so horrendous that even the Pope in Rome tried to stop it, but was intimidated into silence, and Machiavelli, the author of the amoral handbook *The Prince*, denounced the Spanish sovereigns for their "pious cruelty."

We can only speculate what may have happened during these formative years if the Colóns originally came from Majorca. With the

40

edict of 1453, young Columbus may have been baptized Christopher—"Christ bearer"—as part of a genuine or sham conversion by his parents. Alternatively, the family may have fled Majorca, as did many Jews, and sought refuge in Genoa, where they adopted the Italian name Colombo. (Legal records in Genoa of the birth in 1451 and early life of a Cristoforo Colombo, the son of a wool merchant, may refer to a person with a similar name. Alternatively, some historians think the Colón family left Spain as early as 1391 following an anti-Semitic outbreak in Seville and settled in Genoa, adopting the name Colombo and continuing to speak primarily Catalan.) Another possibility is that the Colón family remained in Majorca as New Christians until the *auto da fé* of 1461 prompted them to send young Christopher out of the country by himself. (According to Ferdinand, his father went to sea at age fourteen, which would have been in 1461.) Columbus' later association with Genoa—including several commercial contacts and opening a bank account there in later years—are viewed as part of a plan to have a refuge available for his family should they be persecuted in Spain. As a young man, Columbus served as a mariner under King René of Anjou, the ruler of neighboring Provence where many Jews fled. René was waging a naval war with King John II of Aragon, the father of King Ferdinand and the instigator of the persecution of 1461, and this may have influenced Columbus to serve under his standard.

From his earliest days in Spain, Columbus attracted the attention of the Inquisition. At the first conference in Salamanca to assess his proposal at the Dominican monastery of St. Stephen's, some of the church fathers on the expert commission took offense at his geographical claims which they felt contradicted the Bible. For example, to Columbus' assertion that the earth was spherical, they quoted David in Psalm 103, "Thou stretchest heaven like a hide," indicating that God's terrestrial kingdom was like a curtain or tent-cover constructed by ancient pastoral people from an animal hide, not a round globe. Had not the powerful Cardinal of Toledo intervened on Columbus' behalf at the request of one of the more learned men on the committee, according to a 19th century biographer, "we should have had the spectacle of Christopher Columbus before the terrible Torquemada."

In Spain, Columbus circulated through circles of Jewish or *converso* influence and associated with Jews and Muslims. The tables that he used on his historic voyage were drawn up by Abraham Zacuto, a Jewish astronomer in Salamanca. Joseph Vecinho, another Jew, perfected the instruments he employed. In Spain, Columbus

41

was initially befriended by Diego de Deza, a high churchman of Jewish descent who was tutor to Prince Juan, the heir to the throne. In the New World, Luis de Torres, a Jew who converted just before sailing, served as Columbus' interpreter. Several hundred thousand Spanish Jews were baptized and, as loyal Christians, maintained their commercial interests or high government posts, married into the aristocracy, and even rose to influence in the Church. Tomas Torquemada, the infamous head of the Inquisition, was a New Christian, as was Bartholeme Las Casas, the Franciscan friar who knew Columbus and became the Apostle to the Indies. At Court, Isabella and Ferdinand (who himself reputedly had a Jewish great-grandmother, Paloma of Toledo) were surrounded by advisers, ministers, churchmen, and personal attendants and friends who were born Jewish. The most important *converso* at the time was Luis de Santangel, the royal treasurer to King Ferdinand, a counselor to Queen Isabella, and one of the wealthiest men in Spain. Santangel—whose cousin was burned at the stake for plotting to kill a chief inquisitor—was the one who arranged the audience for Columbus with the monarchs. Also, when the Crown commission rejected Columbus' proposal, it was Santangel who eloquently spoke up on Columbus' behalf and inspired the sovereigns to reverse their decision. Finally, it was Santangel who arranged for the financing of the voyage and to whom Columbus sent his first letter describing his momentous discovery.

In his journal and writings, Columbus frequently refers to his mission in apocalyptic terms. As historians have noted, most of his references are from the Hebrew Bible, rarely from the New Testament. For example, in his journal during the First Voyage, he compared himself to Moses leading the people through the sea to the Promised Land, "So this high sea was very necessary to me, for this had not happened except at the time of the Jews, when they went out of Egypt with Moses who was leading them out of captivity." Elsewhere, Columbus quotes Esdras on a new prophet who will come and lead his people to safety.

Perhaps the most persuasive evidence for the thesis of Columbus' secret Jewish identity is the date of the First Voyage. Columbus set sail from Palos on the early morning of August 3, hours after the deadline expired for the Jews to leave Spain. Following the defeat of the Moors, King Ferdinand and Queen Isabella issued a decree ordering all Jews in Spain to convert to Christianity or leave the country by July 31 (later extended several days because of a religious holiday). The Expulsion—the biggest mass migration of the Jews since

42

the Fall of Jerusalem to the Romans in A.D. 68—caused untold misery and hardship, as hundreds of thousands of people were forced to flee the country and abandon their homes and possessions and leave behind family members who were too old or sick to make the journey. Curiously, Columbus ordered his men to board ship the evening of August 2—the day of the Expulsion—and set sail shortly after sunrise rather than have them board at that time. Whether Columbus deliberately timed his departure to show his solidarity with the uprooted Jews, thumb his nose at authority, or it was pure coincidence, the *Nina, Pinta,* and *Santa Maria* quietly left Spain in the shadow of that fateful day.

Columbus has often been vilified for seeking gold and personal profit. However, in his writings during the First Voyage—before he obtained a single nugget of gold—he observed that his ultimate purpose in obtaining wealth from the East was to outfit a new Crusade to take Jerusalem from the Turks and rebuild Zion. Opening the Holy Land to true believers was a perennial medieval Christian objective, and one that would insinuate him in the good graces of his Catholic sovereigns. However, Columbus' desire to rebuild the Temple (which he referred to, in the Jewish manner, as the Second House) was never a goal of Christendom. On the contrary, it was the age-old dream of the Jews. Spanish Jewry—the Sephardim— saw themselves as descendents of King David, and the original Temple in Jerusalem (the First House) was built by Solomon, his son, according to legend, with gold from Ophir in the East. Columbus'obsessive search for gold suggests that Ophir was his real destination. In the 15th century, one of the most famous prophets of the era, Joachim of Flora, an abbot from South Italy, predicted that "he is to come from Spain who is to recover again the fortunes of Zion." Columbus refers to Joachim in his writings and clearly saw himself —or the Spanish monarchy—as the fulfillment of this prophecy.

Columbus' notebooks, letters to his brothers, and even his signature are cryptic and lend themselves to Kaballistic interpretation. For example, the ciphers in his correspondence with his son Diego may stand for *beEzrat haShem*—"with the help of God—the traditional greeting in Hebrew which some New Christians secretly used among themselves. The theory that Columbus was really seeking the Lost Tribes of Israel or Solomon's lost gold mines to rebuild the Temple—not just the fabled East and its spices—on his voyages cannot be lightly dismissed. Nor can its corollary: that he secretly believed he had found them! There were many striking resemblances between the Indians in Espanola, Cuba, Jamaica, and other islands and the ancient Israelites. The Indians practiced circumcision, avoided touching the dead and tasting blood, observed fast days, married their sisters-in-law if they were childless widows, sacrificed first fruits on mountaintops, and carried a sacred ark before battles. Linguistically, their names for rivers, tools, and foods (including pepper and grain) share roots in common with similar words in Hebrew. While scientists today generally hold these resemblances to be coincidental, early colonists in New England, the Midwest, the Pacific Northwest, and elsewhere commonly believed that native people they encountered descended from the children of Israel.

On the other side of the ledger, there are many passages in his writings, and reports by friends, family, and associates that suggest Columbus was a devout Christian. His private journals, as well as letters to Court, express a deep faith in God and he regularly invoked the blessings of Jesus, Mary, and the saints. He was closely associated with Christian monasteries before and after his voyages and, according to all reports, fervently believed in the evangelization of all people to the saving grace of Christianity. His famous letter to Santangel announcing the success of his First Voyage was couched in the devout imagery of the Holy Faith. As for a pro-Jewish conspiracy or cabal, it should be noted that Columbus' proposal was turned down in Portugal by a three-man council that included two physicians of Jewish descent, and that several of his leading opponents in Castile were *conversos*.

As an emissary on a divine mission, Columbus saw his faith being constantly tested. On the return voyage to Spain in 1493, the ship was in danger of capsizing in a terrific storm and Columbus organized a lottery. Taking a cap, he filled it with chickpeas, including one marked with a cross, and had each crew member select one. The one who selected the marked bean, he explained, would make a pilgrimage on behalf of the entire crew to Our Lady of Guadalupe with a five-pound candle and thank God for causing the storm to cease and bringing them safely to port. Columbus himself drew the marked chickpea. When the storm still did not abate, another lot was held to send a a crew member to Santa Clara of Moguer and hold a mass of thanksgiving, and Columbus again picked the marked bean. The whole crew, meanwhile, vowed to go together to the first church of the Virgin they came to on reaching land. The storm then appeared to halt miraculously and when land was reached, the pledges were redeemed.

# Origin of the Quest

 hatever his origins, in 1476, in his twenties, Columbus joined the crew of a Genoese ship en route to Lisbon. Traveling in a convoy because of naval wars in the Mediterranean, the ship was attacked and sunk off the south coast of Portugal. A strong swimmer, Columbus made it to shore by clinging to an oar and then continued on to Lisbon. Friends from Genoa looked after him and helped him find another seafaring position. On the return from a voyage north, Columbus settled in Lisbon. Portugal was the leading nautical nation of the time. Under Prince Henry the Navigator fifty years earlier, Portuguese captains began making important technological advances and inaugurated the modern age of discovery. Mastering Portuguese, Castilian (the language of neighboring Spain), and Latin (the language of old charts and geography books), Columbus earned his livelihood making maps and charts and selling books.

In 1478, he sailed to Madeira, the port on the Iberian coast, to purchase a cargo of 60,000 pounds of sugar for a Genoese merchant. The following year, he married a local noblewoman, Dona Felipa Perestrello. Her father had been a captain under Prince Henry, and her rank and position enabled her husband to meet high officials. She and Columbus had one son, Diego. Felipa's mother gave Christopher her husband's documents and maps. In 1481 he became a mariner for King John II of Portugal and sailed to the Gold Coast of Africa, halfway down the continent and nearly to the Equator.

During these formative years, Columbus conceived the notion of reaching Asia by sailing west. The precise origin of Columbus' vision is not known, but there are several strands that influenced his thinking. On the voyage north, to Iceland and possibly in sight of Greenland, he may have heard old tales of the Norsemen who reached a large landmass to the west about five hundred years earlier. There was also the chronicle of St. Brenden, the 6th century prelate who was blown off course and reached the Antilles to the southwest before returning to Ireland. Even more fanciful were the legends of devout Christians who had escaped the Islamic invasion of Spain in the 8th century and voyaged west to the Islands of the Seven Cities. The influence of Columbus' father-in-law and his documents and charts was also significant. Most importantly, Colum-

*Nine Star Ki:*
# The Stars He Steered By

We do not know the exact date of Columbus' birth. The conventional date, 1451, would make him a Nine Fire, and Columbus undoubtedly had a lot of active, passionate fire energy."Who can doubt that this fire was not merely mine, but also of the Holy Spirit who encouraged me with a radiance of marvelous illumination . . . urging me to press forward?" he once wrote.

But if we accept his son's account that he was born in 1447, which is more likely, Columbus would have been a Four Tree, which precedes Fire in the Nine Star Ki arrangement but is more stable. In *Nine Star Ki,* an introductory guide to Oriental astrology, Michio Kushi describes the personality of Four Trees:

> 4 Dark Green Tree — This represents the green of older-more matured growth [than young Three Bright Green Tree]. Those born during this year tend to be more thoughtful and practical, and to manifest their idealism in less romantic, more ambitious, or socially oriented goals.
>
> The symbol for this sign is a large, mature tree. Four Tree people are generally of two types. People in the first group are more subdued and have great powers of analysis and strong theoretical ability. They make excellent philosophers, scientists, or administrators, and their contributions are often appreciated by society. Many Nobel Prize winners are among this category. Those in the second category are sensitive to other people's feelings and can embrace many different views. They are idealistic but often lose sight of practicalities, and have a tendency to waste time, energy, and money. Both Four Tree types have a strong desire for freedom and justice, and this can lead them to resist established authority. There are usually eloquent and have the ability to agitate or influence other people. However, they are often indecisive and tend to go along with majority opinion and regret it later. Four Trees often have a hearty laugh and pat other people on the back.
>
> People born under this sign are active in romance. Many Four Tree men are playboy types. They frequently suffer be-

cause of love and tend to get married either very early or very late. They may take financial risks and experience financial insecurity. Four Trees are attracted to administration and management, but are usually disinterested in operational details. They are better at being advisors and guiding the overall direction of an enterprise rather than getting involved with the details of organization.

This description fits Columbus almost perfectly. He was idealistic, eloquent, and visionary, but impractical, financially insecure, and a poor manager. He had a strong sense of justice, but went along with the persecution of Jews and Moors, regretting it at the end of his life. He was also something of a ladies' man and clearly exerted a strong personal magnetism on Queen Isabella.

Asked to describe Columbus' character, the *I Ching* responded with hexagram #11 Peace changing to hexagram #36 Darkening of the Light. The moving line in the second place reads:

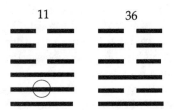

Bearing with the uncultured in gentleness,
Fording the river with resolution,
Not neglecting what is distant,
Not regarding one's companions:
Thus one may manage to walk in the middle.

The commentary explains that this refers to someone with great light or understanding, who by nature is peaceful and gentle, and who is able to bear with imperfect people and avoid factionalism and cliques. This points to Columbus' skill in dealing with pompous and ignorant royal commissions, subduing his mutinous crew, and keeping the peace with the Tainos on his First Voyage. Ultimately, however, he failed miserably as an administrator because he was not strong enough to impose order over multitudes of Spanish colonizers, many of whom were vagabonds, ex-criminals, and battle-hardened veterans of the war against the Moors. Confucius' commentary on hexagram #36 Darkening of the Light describes this final outcome:

Expansion will certainly encounter resistance and injury. . . .
Darkening means damage, injury.
In adversity
It furthers one to be persevering.

On his subsequent voyages, Columbus lost authority, his men rebelled, and he was returned to Spain in fetters. Although freed by the monarchs, he faced adversity for the rest of his life and persevered to clear his name and have his rights fully restored. The *I Ching's* description could not be more accurate.

Interestingly, 1492, the year of Columbus' historic journey, is a Four Tree year and the New World which he encountered, North America, is governed as a whole by Tree energy. Wheat, which Columbus brought on his First Voyage, supplanted corn as the principal grain on the continent. Wheat (governed by upward rising tree energy) creates cultures and civilizations that are strongly idealistic, analytical, and inventive and that govern through ideals and values (e.g., democracy) as opposed to force and power.

Closely associated with Nine Star Ki is the Oriental Zodiac. Columbus was born in a Rabbit year, and people born in this sign are active, outgoing, and energetic and are good at carrying out plans. Like rabbits, they can get off to a fast start, making great leaps and bounds. However, they are by nature gentle, sensitive to criticism, and will do anything to avoid conflict. They are easily intimidated and tend to back down in a confrontation. Also like the proverbial rabbit, after far outdistancing others, they tend to become lazy and in the end may be overtaken. Certainly, this is what happened in Columbus' case, as the race that he launched to colonize the Indies and reap great wealth was ultimately won by others. Even the continents that he discovered were named after someone else!

Unlike other navigators who used a primitive hourglass filled with sand to reckon their position, Columbus counted his own heartbeat. Following his own heart—following his own star in a firmament of darkness and ignorance—became the guiding symbol and metaphor for his historic enterprise.  ❖

*Rival:*
# Amerigo Vespucchi

Amerigo Vespucchi, the Florentine astronomer, merchant, and explorer after whom the Americas are named, was born in 1454, a Six Metal year. Like heaven, the hexagram governing Six energy, Amerigo was strong, active, and untiring. Several years after Columbus' voyage, he sailed west under a Portuguese flag with the object of mapping not only the new lands he might come to but the stars overhead. Like Columbus, who had explored the South American coast on his Third Voyage, Amerigo marveled at the state of uncorrupted nature in which the inhabitants lived and described the topography as a "Terrestrial Paradise."

Amerigo's idyllic description of the native people—especially their lack of property and sovereignty—served as the inspiration for Sir Thomas More's *Utopia* of 1516. His conclusion that the lands he visited might rightly be called "a new world" immortalized his name when Martin Waldseemiller, a continental professor of geography, read an account of Amerigo's voyage, and in 1507 affixed his name to the southern continent he explored on his globe.

In the course of his journey, Amerigo identified the celestial South Pole, discovered longitude, and may have contributed to sending rice to the New World. This grain was first introduced on a large scale in 1512. Like Columbus, Amerigo probably ate rice during his voyage—cats accompanied his voyage to protect grain and other food stores from shipboard rats.

Like Dante, his Florentine mentor who wrote a treatise on world government, Amerigo implicitly criticized the kingdoms and developing colonial empires of his day when he observed that "the lust for possessions, or pillaging, or a desire to rule . . . appear to me to be the cause of wars and every disorderly act."

The roots of the name *Amerigo* itself go back to the Hebrew *amal*, the word for work, and mean one who is "rich through work." Amerigo Vespucci's patient dedication to mapping the heavens; contribution to humanity's vision of utopia, a perfect society on earth; and intermediary for the exchange of foodstuffs between the Old World and New were richly rewarded in the humanistic legacy of the lands that bear his name. ❖

bus obtained a copy of a letter, a drawing of a planisphere, and possibly maps composed by Paolo Toscanelli, a Florentine physician, savant, and mapmaker, who believed in the efficacy of a westward passage. Nicolo de Conti, a 15th century traveler, had lived in Japan for nearly a year and bestowed the name Giappone on that island nation. Conti, a fellow Florentine, inspired Toscanelli's chart. Columbus also read Marco Polo's writings and—like his contemporaries—became fascinated with the Venetian's description of Cathay—the vast Chinese Empire—and the riches of the East. Marco Polo referred to Japan by the name of Cipangu, and as the Gateway to the East, Cipangu became Columbus' original target. He also studied Pierre d'Ailly's *Imago Mundi* (Picture of the World) and the works of classical writers such as Ptolemy, Aristotle, Strabo, Seneca, Pliny, and Solinus whose works contained references to a transoceanic voyage west or a description of the world.

Synthesizing myth and history, legend and Holy Scripture, Columbus combed the Bible and classics for references to the topology of the earth, and from tantalizing allusions and symbols pieced together his own unique geographical conception of the world. He envisioned the circumference of the earth to be smaller than it is and he thought that Asia extended several thousand miles farther west than it does. Prophecy played an increasing role in Columbus' life. In a letter to the King and Queen in 1502, explaining his success, Columbus observed, "I have said that in carrying out the enterprise of the Indies neither reason nor mathematics nor maps was any use to me: fully accountable were the words of Isaiah."

In pursuing his dream, Columbus approached the crowned heads of Europe, hoping to persuade them to finance his expedition. The land routes to the East, at this time, were blocked by the Turks—Constantinople fell in 1453, when he was a small child—and the prospect of opening a new trade route to the fabled wealth of the Orient—including spices, silks, and jewels—was enticing. Contrary to later legend that people of the era believed the earth to be flat, it was known among the learned that the world was round and that the Western Sea connected Europe and Asia. Practically speaking, however, the vessels of that era could sail at Mediterranean latitudes for no more than forty days without making landfall, because the fresh water carried in casks aboard ship was known to turn brackish during this time. (At northern latitudes, water could last about 58 to 59 days.) Provisions and firewood for cooking also dwindled over this six-and-a-half-week period, though fish (and occasionally birds, plants, and other life) from the sea could be obtained to keep a crew alive. However, it was fresh drinking water—or at least a way to preserve it—that marked the limits of the known world.

A closely associated problem was the winds. The square-rigged ships of the day could only sail with the wind at their back or side. Because the winds and ocean currents moved now clockwise, now counterclockwise, this presented a formidable task when heading into the wind. The mariner not only had to take advantage of favorable winds during the voyage, but also had to catch winds moving in an opposite direction on the return. On the open sea at this time, the shortest distance was not a straight line between two points, but often an oblique or spiral motion. Columbus' genius as a navigator lay in mastering the trade winds and in taking advantage of new technology. Earlier pre-Columbian contacts in which isolated European ships reached the Americas were accidental; sailors were blown off course and left to the mercy of the sea. Columbus alone divined the secret of navigating the Atlantic Ocean. Contrary to notion that it was simply luck or Providence that guided him, he had a method—based on dead reckoning, the ability to read the flight of birds, floating debris, and other signs, and the capacity to discriminate between myth and reality in old sea maps and legends—that enabled him to cross uncharted waters. Further, Columbus ordered that lateen sails—flexible triangular sails perfected by the Arabs that allowed ships to take advantage of side and headwinds—be added to the *Nina* and *Pinta*. This technological advance gave the expedition increased maneuverability and speed on its historic journey.

In 1484 Columbus approached King John II of Portugal, but a royal committee rejected his plan as unsound. Later, the Portuguese monarch outfitted a ship to carry out a voyage similar to Columbus', but it became stranded. (Columbus did not disclose his sailing method to the Portuguese, nor later to the Spanish, because he feared, rightly, that his plan would be stolen.) Meanwhile, Dona Felipe, Columbus' young wife, died, and he left Portugal to find support elsewhere. In Spain, he left Diego, his son, at a Franciscan monastery in La Rábida. Influential friends and contacts arranged an audience for Columbus with the Spanish King and Queen. However, in an era of brutal wars—civil, foreign, and religious—launching such a quixotic expedition appeared the height of folly. Columbus' grandiose demands, including a share of any wealth he obtained and the hereditary title of Admiral of the Ocean Sea and viceroy of all islands and continents he claimed in the name of the sovereigns, marked him as a social climber as well as a dreamer, and his request was tabled. In Córdoba, Columbus' second son, Ferdinand, was born, and raised by Beatriz Enríquez de Harana, a young woman whom he never married.

On a visit to Portugal, Columbus learned that Bartholomew Diaz, one of the greatest mariners of the era, had just returned from the Cape of Good Hope at the tip of southern Africa. His discovery—signifying that an eastern sea route to Asia lay open—caused the Portuguese to lose interest in sponsoring a westward expedition. Despite these rebuffs, Columbus continued to lobby at the court of Queen Isabella and King Ferdinand. Rulers of the new combined states of Castille and Aragon, the Spanish monarchs were engaged in a protracted war with the Moors. For six years, Columbus remained in Spain, pursuing his dream. Finally, in the flush of victory over the Moors and the fall of Granada in 1492, the Spanish rulers could afford to be more generous and, after intensive politicking, agreed to sponsor Columbus' expedition. From Palos, a harbor town that furnished two of his three ships, Columbus set sail on August 3, 1492. Two and a half months later, he set foot on an island off what he believed to be the mainland of Asia.

## The Voyages

 fter a layover in the Canary Islands to repair a broken rudder and restock water and provisions, Columbus' expedition sailed west on September 9. As the days passed without sight of land, the crew grew increasingly restless—indeed mutinous—and the captain had to use all of his understanding of human psychology, as well as authority, to keep his men in line. On one occasion, Columbus observed a specimen of seaweed that he had never seen before and called it to the attention of his crew. "The grasses are more numerous," he recorded in his journal. "Many were seen and very often; they were rock-weeds and they came from the west . . . from morning on, they were seen in abundance and they appeared to come from some river." To quiet the crew, Columbus kept two nautical journals, one showing what he thought to be the true distance traversed, the other showing a much more optimistic estimate which he shared with the crew. With the instruments available at the time, sailors could not measure longitude or East-West distance with precision.

On October 2, seaweed again played a critical role in mollifying the anxiety of his shipmates, when Columbus pointed out seaweed moving from east to west in the turbid waters, contrary to the usual flow. On October 8, "the sea of grass"—the Sargasso Sea infamous for entangling ships in thick seaweed—ended, and Columbus' ships encountered clear water amid the masses of wrack and tangle.

On October 11 the crew sighted a piece of bamboo and what appeared to be carved pieces of wood. That night, about 10 p.m., Columbus thought he saw a light—like a flickering candle—in the distance. At 2:00 A.M. on October 12, Juan Rodriguez Bormejo, a seaman aboard the *Pinta*, sighted land. Columbus and his crew disembarked, knelt on the sand, and claimed the island in the name of the Spanish monarchs. Columbus named the island San Salvador—Holy Savior. The Indian name for it was Guanahani—Isle of Iguanas. Believing he had landed in the Indies, Columbus called the inhabitants *Indians*. Modern day anthropologists refer to them as the Tainos. They spoke Arawak, as did the Caribs, a neighboring tribe, and other cultures in the islands, and their ancestors originally lived in the Orinoco Valley and the Amazonia region of South America and settled in the Caribbean several millennia earlier.

The most impressive thing about the natives, Columbus marveled, was their gentleness, friendliness, and peacefulness. They were so innocent of war and weaponry that one man who asked to see a sword clasped the blade and drew blood.

The natives brought the Spanish food and water. One man was carrying with him "a piece of their bread, about as large as the fist, and a gourd of water, and a piece of brown earth, powdered and then kneaded [chocolate], and dried leaves," Columbus recorded. In turn, he ordered that wheat bread, honey, and molasses be given to the natives. They also gave the natives glass beads, bells, and other ornaments.

Turning his attention to the natural landscape, Columbus wrote Ferdinand and Isabella: "Your Highnesses may believe that this is the best and most fertile and temperate and level and good land that there is in the world." On his tour of the island, Columbus turned his keen eye to inventorying the crops and foodstuffs of the inhabitants. These included a wide variety of herbs, purslane, wild amaranth, beans, pumpkins "sown on a mountain," something like barley "sown in a valley," various fish, sweet potatoes, and *niames* [yams]. This latter, he discovered, served as the principal staple of the islanders. "[E]ach of them brought to [us] what they had to eat, which is bread of '*niames*,' that is, or roots like large carrots which

# Soulmate:
# Queen Isabella

Queen Isabella is known as the Mother of the Americas. Unlike her husband, King Ferdinand, she enthusiastically supported Columbus' mission and he, in turn, idolized her. From the Nine Star Ki perspective, this is easy to understand. Isabella, born in 1451, was a Nine Fire, and the glamor, wealth, and spiritual glory to be won by a successful westward passage to the East and conversion of the unbaptized appealed to her active, passionate character. The King, born in 1452, was an Eight Soil, more passive, thoughtful, and unyielding like the mountain that symbolizes this energy in the *I Ching*. Columbus' Four Tree energy, moreover, supported Isabella's fiery nature, but conflicted with Ferdinand's more earthbound personality.

Describing the Queen's appearance and character, Hernando del Pulgar, her private secretary, wrote: "This Queen was of middle height, well made in her person and in the proportion of her limbs, very white and fair; her eyes between green and blue, her glance graceful and modest, the features of her face well set, her face very beautiful and gay. She was well measured in the countenance and movements of her person; she drank no wine, she was a very good woman and liked to have old women of good lineage and character beside her."

Because of palace intrigues, Isabella grew up in the countryside, according to a modern biographer, "amid rolling hills, grazing sheep, and fields of wheat, oats, and barley rather than . . . the elegant banquets, mimes, and jousts of a royal court." Her strong constitution, nourished on a simple diet, prepared her well, physically and spiritually, to govern. As Queen of Castile, the larger of the two kingdoms, she overshadowed her husband and personally oversaw the consolidation of her domains.

These yang qualities developed, not only amidst the Darwinian struggle for survival among 15th century royalty, but also as a result of the rich animal food she began to partake since assuming power. Court food customarily consisted of tureens and plates of wild boar, venison, salmon, and other strong meats; swans, peacocks, and other delicate fare; fresh cheese, puff pastries, and other sumptuous desserts. Isabella may have retained a special liking for chicken which served as the centerpiece of her wedding banquet. The depopulation of hens for that occasion left "all the cocks . . . looking frightfully lonely," we read in a contemporary account.

On the field of battle, Isabella earned the reputation as a Joan of Arc ministering to her troops. She inspired soldiers into battle against the Moors, planned strategy, and served as quartermaster, overseeing provisions of food for her armies. Though she would have liked to have shared the life of an ordinary soldier, she lived and dined in the sumptuous scale which was expected of her. On one campaign, she was feted "with a magnificent meal of white bread, poultry and other meats, fruit, pastries made of sugar and honey, fine wines and sweet-smelling water, all of which were served on golden, bejeweled plates."

In rooting out heretics, she subscribed to the principles of Cardinal Borgia: "We have always striven to apply suitable remedies for the wretched folly of those people as for a pernicious disease." In addition to surgical removal of her enemies, she set up the first military field hospitals so that medical operations could be conducted on the battlefield.

Surgery proved to be Isabella's epitaph as well as triumph. The last years of her life saw the tragic deaths of her son, Juan, the heir to her throne; her grandson; and her daughter. These reversals are known in Spanish history as the Three Knives of Sorrow. Shortly thereafter, another daughter, Juana, the surviving heir, went insane. Isabella herself died from a lingering, painful sickness—possibly cancer, as a tumor is mentioned. (Dairy food probably played a role in her final illness, as her plump visage indicates.)

Queen Isabella was a brilliant political ruler, efficient administrator, and victorious military strategist. She also had the imagination to back Columbus' quixotic voyage and, to her credit, valiantly opposed extension of slavery into the New World. However, a life of rich food largely cost her the physical and spiritual gifts that she inherited, and, in place of honor, glory, and radiance, she left Spain with a legacy of unspeakable cruelty and shame.                                                                    ❖

they grow, for they sow and grow and cultivate this in all these lands, and it is their mainstay of life." The *niames* tasted something like chestnuts and Columbus pronounced them very savory. The people also made a bread of *niames* called *ajes*, "which is very white and good," and enjoyed *cacubi*, a bread made from the root of the yucca or cassava plant.

As a beverage, they enjoyed *chufa*, a small tuber from a reedlike plant from which they extracted a refreshing drink, white in color and nutty in taste.

The natives had kind hearts, Columbus observed, giving all they had. "On this day, more than 120 canoes came to the ships, all being full of people, and they all brought something, especially their bread and fish, and water in small earthenware jars, and seeds of many kinds, which are good spices," wrote Bartolome de Las Casas, the Dominican friar who subsequently chronicled Columbus' account from lost logbooks and became the chief defender of the Indians against Spanish cruelty. "They threw a grain into a mug of water and drank it, and the Indians, whom the Admiral carried with him, said that it was a most healthy thing."

From San Salvadore, Columbus sailed to other islands in the Bahamas, which he named Santa Maria de la Concepcion, Fernandina, and Isabella. Pushing on further south, he arrived at Cuba which he named Juana. (Note his sense of order, naming the islands respectively for Jesus, Mary, the King, the Queen, and the Crown Prince of Spain.) Searching for gold and other precious metals, Columbus asked the Indians at each encounter where such mineral wealth could be obtained. They brought a few trinkets, but nothing of substance was discovered. In Hispaniola, the natives indicated that there was a goldmine in the interior. On Christmas day, 1492, the *Santa Maria* went aground and had to be abandoned. From the timbers of his flagship, Columbus had a small fort built which he called La Navidad (Nativity). Enflamed by tales of gold, some of the crew asked to remain as colonists, and thirty-nine stayed when Columbus departed.

The *Niña* and the *Pinta* sailed for home on January 16, 1493. After a frightful voyage, in which the ships almost capsized in a raging storm, Columbus arrived off the Iberian coast. In Barcelona, King Ferdinand and Queen Isabella welcomed Columbus, and he presented them with several gold trinkets, exotic parrots and other plants and animals, some cloth and utensils from the New World, and six Tainos that he had taken back with him. The monarchs bestowed upon Columbus the titles that he had requested and showered him with honors.

Columbus made three subsequent voyages. In 1493, he returned with seventeen ships and 1,200 men and stayed for nearly three years. In Hispaniola, the Spanish found that La Navidad, the first colony, had been burned and the seamen left behind slain. Columbus authorized a new colony to be established and explored the coasts of Jamaica, Cuba, and Hispaniola. Cattle, sheep, pigs, goats, dogs, and chickens were imported, and the local inhabitants were forced to work as virtual slaves and provide an exorbitant amount of gold. This harsh plantation system—later known as the *encomienda*—was ruthlessly enforced. Many natives were murdered or tortured as examples to the others, and entire native communities were put to the sword or committed suicide to avoid their fate. The harsh treatment meted out by Columbus and his brothers was not directed exclusively at native peoples. The Spanish colonizers were severely punished for infractions and many were hanged. By the end of his Second Voyage, Columbus fell dangerously ill. For weeks, he suffered high fever, a delirium, coma, and constant pain.

In 1498, on his Third Voyage, Columbus sighted Trinidad and explored the northeastern part of South America and the Leeward Islands. Meanwhile, many colonists rebelled at his dictatorial rule and complained to the sovereigns back in Spain. A new governor was appointed who had Columbus arrested and returned to Spain in chains. The King and Queen later ordered the Admiral released and restored his titles, but left the effective management of the Indies to others.

On his final voyage in 1500, Columbus tried to find a passage to the Asian mainland, convinced he was on the periphery of China. He lost two ships on an expedition to Central America and his remaining two ships capsized off Jamaica. Fortunately, messengers sent by canoe reached Hispaniola, and Columbus was rescued in 1504. Columbus' health declined during this last voyage, and he returned to Spain sick and disheartened. Queen Isabella, his main patron, had died, and King Ferdinand remained noncommittal to his claims. Columbus died in Valladolid, Spain, on May 20, 1506. In his last days, he turned his attention to recovering his authority and honors and to mystical pursuits.

# Clash of Cultures—and Cuisines

he Encounter—as historians now call it—between Columbus and the inhabitants of the Western Hemisphere was a clash of cultures, perceptions of the world, and ways of life. From the modern view, the Spanish Conquest of the Caribbean and eventually parts of North, Central, and South America was a civilizing force, a necessary evil to bring primitive cultures into the modern world, a triumph of religion, morality, and good taste over human sacrifice, cannibalism, and stone age technology. From the view of the conquered peoples and their descendents, the arrival of Columbus and his successors was an unmitigated disaster, leading to centuries of oppression and degradation which have not yet entirely been lifted.

From the perspective of Oriental medicine and philosophy, the compass of yin and yang can help us understand the dynamics of the Encounter. Relative to each other, the Spanish were extremely yang—strong, commanding, passionate, aggressive, and zealous. The Tainos, in contrast, were extremely yin—gentle, accommodating, passive, and leisure-loving.

Climate, geography, and weather help to explain part of the differences between the two cultures. Castile, the populous heartland of Spain, was mountainous, with dry air, and rivers that tended to dry up in the summer. In contrast, the Caribbean islands were tropical paradises with gentle breezes and little temperature change. These environmental differences created radically different ways of eating, as the Pope recognized in the Papal Bull of 1493 (quoted at the head of this chapter) in which he awarded Spain possession of the Indies as much by dietary preference as by divine right. As ruler of Christendom, the Pontiff assumed that representatives of a strong animal-food eating civilization enjoyed the natural right to govern weak people—"naked, vegetarian."

The Spanish, like most Europeans, were a heavy meat-eating society. King Alfonso X, the ancestor of Ferdinand and Isabella, put it well in his discourse on *The Praise of Spain*:

> Spain is abundant in her harvests, delightful in her fruit, extravagant in her fish, savory in her milk and in all the things which are made from milk; full of game, covered with cattle, happy in her

houses, comfortable in her mules, safe and well provided with castles, merry with good wines, easy in her abundance of bread; rich in metals, lead, tin, quicksilver, iron, copper, silver, gold, precious stones, marble, sea salts and land salt-mines and salt-rock and many other mines . . . proud of her silk and all that is made of it; sweet with honey and sugar, lighted by her wax, plentiful in oil, gay with saffron.

In contrast, the Tainos and other native cultures, like most traditional people, were a semi-vegetarian culture, subsisting primarily on root crops, tubers, vegetables, and fruit. The principal food in the Bahamas and Caribbean islands was *niames* (yams), cassava (yuca), wild amaranth, sweet potatoes, peppers, squash, and beans. Native people ate a small volume of animal food, especially fish and seafood, but also occasionally ducks and other fowl, turtles, iguana, rabbit, and a type of barkless dog. As Las Casas cynically observed, the Spanish ate more in one day than the Indians ate in a month.

Columbus recognized the central importance of diet in settling and developing the new lands. In a memorandum he wrote upon returning to Spain, he emphasized the need to export foods to the islands from Europe so that future settlers would not become sick. "The preservation of health depends upon [our] people being provided with the food to which they are accustomed in Spain, for none of them, or others who may newly arrive, can serve their highnesses unless they are in health."

Later, in the same directive, he noted that the Spanish would need to import animals to the Indies to provide food:

Though we have enough biscuit, as well as corn [wheat], for some while, yet it is necessary that some reasonable amount should also be sent . . . and likewise some salt meat, I mean bacon, and other salt flesh, which would be better than that which we have brought on this voyage. As to livestock sheep and lambs [are needed] above all, more females than males, and some calves and young heifers are necessary, so that they should come always in every caravel which may be sent here . . . Of these things we have already great need, such as of raisins, sugar, almonds, honey and rice, of which a great quantity should have come and very little arrived, and that which did come [already] has been expended and consumed.

Uprooted from their native farmland, the Tainos died out within a generation of Columbus' landing. In addition to slavery and massacre, their fate was sealed by the spread of epidemics. Lacking immunity to smallpox and other European scourges, the native population on Hispaniola, for example, declined from an estimated 500,000 men and women in 1492 to 60,000 in the census of 1509, 11,000 in 1518, and by 1550 it was extinct. Altogether several million native peoples in the Caribbean are believed to have perished in the wake of Columbus' voyages. In 1510, King Ferdinand sent 250 black Africans, purchased at a slave mart in Lisbon, to the Caribbean to replace native workers who had all but died out. Thus the African slave trade was introduced into the Americas.

By later standards, the actual amount of meat and animal food consumed by the Spanish sailors and settlers was modest. A manifest of food aboard the *Nina* on its voyage of 1498 gives a glimpse of the actual diet Columbus and his crew ate. The ship carried 34 *cahizes* (17 tons) of wheat, 2 cahizes of garbanzo beans, 4375 pounds of flour, 100 *quintals* of biscuit, 2377 pounds of cheese, 2450 pounds of salt pork, 625 pounds of pigs' feet, 1/4 ton of sardines, and smaller amounts of olive oil, wine, vinegar, and raisins. The main food aboard ship was an unleavened bread, which was baked in a stove on the forecastle.

By weight, grain constituted about 60 percent of the food cargo, beans 10 percent, and animal food only 10 percent. By proportion, this compared favorably with the traditional diet of humanity, which generally consisted of from 50 to 60 percent whole cereal grains, 20 to 30 percent vegetables, 10 percent beans and sea vegetables, and 5 to 10 percent animal food. The biggest difference was the lack of fresh vegetables—a perennial nutritional deficiency in ships' rations until the advent of refrigeration. However, since none of the crew contracted scurvy, Columbus apparently stocked up on fresh fruits and vegetables in the Canaries that were not recorded on the original Spanish manifest.

By category and volume of foods, the Spanish diet and the native Caribbean diet were not so radically different as we might imagine. The principal difference was in the amount of salt consumed. The cheese, pork, sardines, and other animal food eaten by the Spanish were preserved in large amounts of salt, as was meat and poultry generally through the Middle Ages and Renaissance. Salt, the most contracting or yang, of usual foodstuffs in the human diet, is essential to health and vitality. However, too much salt creates extremely active, aggressive, potentially violent behavior and a mind that is hard, rigid, and unyielding. Such was the way of life and way of thinking of many Europeans in the Middle Ages and Age of Discovery. In addition, bread and other baked goods, including ships' rations, or hardtack—recall Shakespeare's "as dry as the remainder biscuit"—are extremely yang. Not surprisingly, seamen living on a diet of salted meat and fish and baked grain, coupled with a lack of good quality yin, were among the most yang segments of society. (Traditionally, seamen were known as "old salts," and in most empires from Elizabethan and Victorian England to Imperial Japan the navy was more dominant and aggressive than the army.) Despite a relatively small amount of animal food consumption (10 percent versus 20 to 30 percent in present day society), the quality of the meat, cheese, and other animal products consumed, as well as bread and hard, dry biscuits, yielded the active, dynamic, adventurous, but often brutal and sadistic character that we associate with the Conquistadors and their successors.

The violence and plunder that Spain introduced into the New World were rife at home. Generations of internecine conflict and bloodshed had wracked Iberia's ten kingdoms. Crime, rape, arson, and massacre stalked the land and had only recently declined because of the harsh justice of the new King and Queen who had unified the largest kingdoms and defeated the Moors. In light of future assimilation between the Spanish and the cultures they vanquished, a strong case can be made that the destruction of New World cultures was not so much racially motivated, as it was the result of a modernizing trend that had spiraled out of control. In contrast to Spain and Portugal and their overseas empires, northern European societies, especially Britain and Germany, disapproved of intermarriage with native peoples and developed ideologies of racial superiority to justify their rule. This difference once again is primarily dietary. The northern Protestant countries were more yang, eating more salt and animal food and less whole grains and vegetables, while the southern Catholic states were eating more grains, beans, vegetables, fruit, and other more moderate fare, as well as more oil and spices, available in sunny Mediterranean latitudes.

# Columbus' Health and Diet

nformation about Columbus' own way of eating is meager. Evaluating his constitution and condition from descriptions and likenesses, however, enables us to make some tentative conclusions about his diet and its effect on his character and destiny. "The Admiral was a well-built man of more than average stature, the face long, the cheeks somewhat high, his body neither fat nor lean," Ferdinand, his son, wrote. "He had an aquiline nose and light-colored eyes; his complexion too was light and tending to bright red. In youth his hair was blond, but when he reached the age of thirty, it all turned white." "In eating and drinking, and in the adornment of his person, he was very moderate and modest," he continued. "He was affable in conversation with strangers and very pleasant to the members of his household, though with a certain gravity. He was so strict in matters of religion that for fasting and saying prayers he might have been taken for a member of a religious order. . . . And so fine was his hand that he might have earned his bread by that skill alone."

Las Casas confirmed this description: "His form was tall, above the medium: his face long and his countenance imposing: his nose aquiline: his eyes clear blue: his complexion light, tending toward a decided red: his beard and hair were red when he was young, but which cares then had early turned white." Oviedo, another contemporary, recorded: "He was of good stature and appearance, of more than medium height and with strong limbs, his eyes bright and his other features of good proportion: his hair very red and his face somewhat burned and freckled."

These qualities indicate that Columbus had a strong constitution inherited from his parents. His native strength and vitality and well-proportioned body further show that he came from hardy stock derived from generations of grain-eating ancestors. His blond or red hair, light complexion and blue eyes, are strong yang traits, showing that his parents and grandparents also ate animal food and a lot of bread and salt. In contrast, height is basically a conditional trait that depends upon our daily way of eating after birth. Tallness is more yin, indicating that as a child and youth Columbus ate proportionately more yin foods than average such as milk, fruit, sugar, and spices.

As a young man, Columbus was quiet and meditative, further showing that he had a more yin, gentle character. Columbus' life-long mystical streak and penchant for secrecy, prophecy, and hidden meanings—strong yin characteristics—signify that he likely ate a good deal of honey throughout his life. Honey creates a dreamy, fanciful mind given to esoteric pursuits and quests. People—like bees—who eat a lot of honey become strongly attracted to a Queen Bee around whom their life revolves. In Columbus' case, this was clearly Queen Isabella, his patron and sovereign, whom he idolized and devoted all of his energies. Columbus named one of the first islands he visited Isabella and he named the first town he founded in the New World, Isabella, after her. There are numerous references to honey in his journals, as we have already noted, and there are other indications that this sweet fare influenced his perceptions. On the tour of one island he visited, Columbus noted that the mountain that he had just climbed looked like a large beehive. On a later voyage, he compared his ship to a colony of bees, observing that it was "more perforated by worms than a honeycomb." There are numerous references to Columbus offering native rulers biscuits and honey to eat, and his well-known freckles resulted—not directly from the sun itself—but from too much honey, fruit, and other simple sugar intake (i.e., excessive yin factors) that exposure to the sun (yang) drew out.

No portraits of Columbus drawn or painted from life are known to exist. Most early likenesses appear to draw on the descriptions of family and associates quoted above. The earliest—commissioned by Paolo Giovio, a wealthy historian, for his villa—shows Columbus with curly gray hair that is thin and receding (see frontispiece to this chapter). The nose is long and aquiline, the brows downward turning, the mouth tight, and the lower lip swollen, especially on the left side. The eyes are sad and downcast, a striking countenance attributed by art critics to the picture being composed after the disastrous Third Voyage. The modest, almost penitential robes he is wearing lend credence to this interpretation. A woodcut of the original painting appeared in 1575, and most subsequent artistic impressions have been based on it.

From these brief descriptions and likenesses, it would appear that Columbus was endowed with a strong physical and mental constitution. This yang inheritance—aggravated by animal food, bread, and salt in his daily diet—in turn attracted him to yin. As a child and young man, he probably developed a sweet tooth and acquired a more gentle, peaceful, artistic yin character. As a sailor and later sea captain, he was attracted to the Orient and the mysterious world of mastic, spices, and sugar—all extremely yin. Sampling some of these expansive foods, especially honey, he began daydreaming about fabulous wealth and power—much like children and adults today, who eating hamburgers, pizza, ice cream and soft drinks, are easily susceptible to entering realms of fantasy while watching soap operas on television, playing video or computer games, or betting compulsively on the lottery. Like Don Quixote, the knight-errant in Cervantes' later novel, Columbus tilted at windmills and lived in sand castles of his own imagination. But blessed with good looks, a sweet disposition, and a mellifluous voice, he was able to attract others to his cause.

The practical demands of being a sailor and facing very real challenges and obstacles on the high seas grounded Columbus and served him as well as his eloquence and honeyed speech. The strong yang, salty diet aboard ship tempered his illusions and gave him the power and perseverance to realize his ambitions. It also caused his hair to turn prematurely gray. By the time Columbus settled in Spain and approached the Queen and King, his diet and experience presented an unusual blend of yin and yang qualities. He had a big dream and practical know how, he was both firm and yielding, he was brave and foolhardy. He reconciled within himself the opposites that were rendering asunder Spain and the rest of Renaissance Europe.

Over the years, Columbus trained himself to become a skilled observer of people and life on land, as well as sea. Physiognomy played an important role at several points in his career. On his trip to Ireland, he reported seeing several persons adrift in a boat who had flat faces and other Oriental features. In Guinea, he studied the physiognomy of the African people. On the first day of his landing, on October 12, the explorer keenly observed the features and appearance of the islanders. He wrote the monarchs, "They love their neighbors as themselves, and they have the softest and gentlest voice in the world and are always smiling."

Accepting the natives' hospitality, Columbus and his men began to eat native foods, especially cassava, sweet potatoes, and other more yin fare. As their journey continued, their health improved. "Praise be to Our Lord," Columbus recorded in his log in November about six weeks after landing, "so far there has not been a single one of my people who has had a headache or who had been in bed because of sickness, except for one old man through pain from kidney stones, from which he has suffered all his life—and even he became well at the end of two days."

As for the Tainos' reaction to Spanish food, Columbus gives a hint. "I gave the King some of our Castilian food. He ate a mouthful and afterward gave the rest to his advisers and to the governor and the others who were with him." Other references like this in which the natives sampled what is offered may be viewed as simply good manners and a spirit of sharing. Or considering how they never took more than a taste, this may suggest that the Tainos found the food too extreme or unappetizing, but were too polite to refuse it. As for the visitors' appearance, the islanders remarked among themselves on the Spaniards' pale complexions and hairy bodies. The fact the Tainos ran away and were clearly frightened suggests that the Europeans' large, heavy physiques, fearsome countenances, and general noisiness (including periodic firing of muskets and cannon) contrasted sharply with their own softer, more yin temperament and disposition.

Physiognomy also played a key role on Columbus' Second Voyage when he gave credence to reports of cannibalism among the Caribs by observing the faces of several tribesmen and reporting that their "deranged" features confirmed his worst suspicions.

## The Hidden Dietary Factor

 olumbus' probable Jewish ancestry helps to explain several mysterious facets of his character and development. The difference between Christians and Jews in the High Middle Ages and Renaissance was not simply a matter of faith. It was a matter of diet and health. For thousands of years, the Jewish people had kept to a dietary code known as *kasreth* or *kosher* as described in the Bible. This involved stringent laws regarding the cooking and consumption of certain foods. Historically, this code represented a compromise between a nomadic and urban way of life through which the Hebrew people passed in their sojourn in Mesopotamia, Egypt, and Palestine. As they became more settled people, developing agriculture and living in cities, animal food became less and less a central part of the Israelite diet. Especially in a hot, warm climate, animal food taken on a regular basis is detrimental to usual good health.

The kosher laws regarding the slaughter and mixing of foods, for example milk and meat, can be seen as both a hygienic code to protect against disease and as a method to minimize or reduce the amount of animal food intake altogether. (The entire phenomena of animal sacrifice during this era may have been an attempt by the priests and prophets of Israel to discourage animal food consumption by offering the first and best portions to the deity as well as imprint upon people's minds the solemnity of taking life.)

During the Diaspora, Jews continued to observe the dietary code, eating unleavened bread on Passover, using two sets of dishes for cooking and serving, and observing other rules of purity. Though not vegetarian, the Jewish way of eating included more grains and vegetable-quality foods than the medieval Christian diet. Following the collapse of the Roman Empire, Europe had fragmented into a patchwork of feudal kingdoms and principalities (such as the various states that were united in Spain by Ferdinand and Isabella). The network of granaries developed by the Romans, along with a reliable and efficient transportation system, collapsed, and whole grains could no longer be moved easily across Europe to make up for poor harvests, blight, or other shortages. Also a mini-Ice Age set in, making for longer, colder winters. As a result, Europeans began to eat proportionately more animal food and to kill their livestock to survive the winters. Previously, as in Asia, cattle and other farm animals in Europe were used primarily for plowing, transport, and labor. The amount of animal food consumed in medieval Europe soared, creating a stronger, more physically active population, but also a more rigid, inflexible mind. This is the underlying biological reason behind the violence, prejudice, and intolerance of the Middle Ages, culminating in the Dark Ages, the Crusades, and the Inquisition.

Extremes of meat (yang) and sugar and spices (yin) created a dualistic mentality that separated heaven from earth, mind from body, reason from faith. Nowhere was this more pronounced than in Spain, with its vast Castilian plains devoted to cattle ranching. The cattle culture that developed in Spain served as the embryonic model for the entire New World, including the cowboys of the American West and the *gauchos* of Latin America. Along with the seamen and navigators, the Spanish cattle culture represented one of the most yang elements in society.

Forbidden to own land or farm, the Jews were not a direct part of the beef, dairy, or bull-fighting complex. Also, because of their Levantine heritage, they were more attuned to the traditional Mediterranean way of life and eating. Unlike the Christians, who used lard in cooking, the Jews traditionally used vegetable oil to cook their foods. They commonly enjoyed stews made with onions and garlic; and telltale evidence of vegetable oil in their stockpots, abstaining from pork, or using separate dishes for animal food was sometimes used against New Christian families by the Inquisition to show that they were secretly practicing Jewish ways. Honey particularly played a festive role. On Rosh Ha-Shannah, the Jewish New Year, for example, bread was customarily dipped into honey as a token of the sweet year ahead. Apple pieces were also dipped in honey accompanied by the prayer: "May it be Thy will O Lord our God and God of our fathers to renew unto us a good and sweet year."

In the final Edict of Expulsion, King Ferdinand and Queen Isabella cited dietary lapse as one of the chief offenses:

> . . . We are informed by the Inquisitors and by many other religious persons, ecclesiastical and secular, it is evident and apparent that the great damage to the Christians has resulted from and does result from the participation, conversation, and communication that they have had with the Jews, who try to always achieve by whatever ways and means possible to subvert and to draw away faithful Christians from our holy Catholic faith and to separate them from it, and to attract and pervert them to their injurious belief and opinion, instructing them in their ceremonies and observances of the Law, . . . notifying them of Passover before it comes, advising them what they should observe and do for it, giving them and taking unto them the unleavened bread and the slaughtered meats with their ceremonies, instructing them on the things they should stay away from, thus in the foods as in the other matters . . .

In Columbus' case, we can speculate that, at least in his early years, his formative diet was more plant-oriented as a result of Jewish influence. Later, as a professing New Christian, he may have swung in the other direction. However, years of poverty and difficulty suggest that his way of eating in the years prior to his First Voyage was plain and simple. Arriving in Spain penniless, Columbus begged bread for his small son and himself at a monastery. In fact, according to contemporaries, he was so poor that he wore threadbare clothes and "had not a pot to cook in." Rice and beans, the staple of the poor, then as today, was probably Columbus' main food during the time he conceived his mission as well as the long years winning the allegiance of the King and Queen. And the rice—

# *I Ching:*
# Crossing the Great Water

The real Father of the Americas was Luis de Santangel, the accomplished financier and courtier, who introduced Columbus to Isabella, convinced her to override the expert commission which rejected his theory, and underwrote the journey when Queen Isabella, persuaded by Columbus' eloquence and nobel bearing, impulsively pledged her jewels to finance the expedition to the Indies. Santangel was born into a Jewish family and converted to Christianity, but like many New Christians he retained sympathy for his old faith, helping to protect Jews from the Inquisition and later helping them as exiles to leave Spain.

Was Columbus—who attracted the attention of the Inquisition at the first presentation of his enterprise to the assembled churchmen and scholars—Jewish? Consulting the *I Ching* for insight into this matter, I received the hexagram #59 Dispersion changing to #61 Inner Truth.

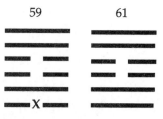

Dispersion signifies a situation of imminent dissolution and separation. The judgment declares:

Dispersion. Success.
The king approaches his temple.
It furthers one to cross the great water.
Perseverance furthers.

On the one hand, the dispersion refers to Columbus' proposed Expedition to the Indies which was in danger of collapse. On the other, it can also be viewed as referring to the approaching expulsion of the Jews, which was being actively considered by the monarchs at the same time they were pondering Columbus' venture. In addition to the horrors of the Inquisition, the Jews of Spain now faced forced exile from the land in which they had lived for over a millennium. To thwart this catastrophe, the leaders of the Jewish community and their New Christian supporters latched onto Columbus' idea. Perhaps they could transmute their monarchs' religious fanaticism into a far-flung quest for material riches and, in return for sponsoring such an expedition, reap merit or a longer grace period for their co-religionists and themselves.

The crux of the matter is signified in the moving, or changing, lines in the *I Ching*. In hexagram 59 received above, there is one moving line in the first place which reads, "He brings help with the strength of a horse. Good fortune." Confucius' traditional commentary states:

> The strong horse is the nine in the second place. K'an means a strong horse with a beautiful back. The six at the beginning is weak and in a lowly place, and does not itself possess the strength to stop the dissolution. But the since the line is only at the beginning of the dissolution, its rescue is relatively easy. The strong, central nine in the second place comes to its aid, and the six submits and joins with it in service to the ruler in the fifth place.

The lowly six at the beginning is clearly Columbus, the strong central nine who comes to his rescue is Santangel (who, incidentally, was a knight, or strong horse), and the ruler is Isabella. Some historians have hinted at this scenario. In 1492: *The Decline of Medievalism and the Rise of the Modern Age*, Barnet Litvinoff writes:

> If history requires a parallel to the biblical Joseph at Pharoah's court, Santangel is surely that man. From an obscure origin he had risen to statesman's rank, a Hispanic Jew endowed with great wealth, as devout a Catholic as any, yet acknowledging to his conscience an obligation towards the Israelite connection. The sentence hanging over the Jews weighed heavily

upon him as he tendered his counsel to the royal couple. . . . As Santangel viewed the situation, Christopher Columbus allowed the possibility of diverting the fanatical rhetoric of Torquemada [the Grand Inquisitor]. The latter preached an apocalyptic cause: the destruction of the Muslim state was not enough, nor the rigorous exposure of Jews secretly performing Satan's work while masquerading as Christians. This nation would be Catholic or it would be nothing. And so, in the course of the year 1491, the banishment of the Jews grew from a mood to a proposal, then to a divine injunction. . . . Luis himself had nothing to fear because of his closeness to [King] Ferdinand, who protected him and his children. But the Jews' situation continued to hang on a thread, simultaneously with the fate of Columbus.

In *The Jews of Spain,* Jane S. Gerber reminds us that the Inquisition cast its shadow over the Santangels. Members of Luis de Santangel's family were burned alive for plotting to assassinate the Inquisitor, others were burned in effigy, and on July 17, 1491, the year before Columbus sailed, his son and namesake, Luis, was accused of Judaizing and forced to wear a *sambenito* (a hooded cloak) in a public processional of penitence. "Perhaps Santangel, reeling from the devastation wreaked upon his family by the long arm of the Inquisition, was animated more by personal than by scientific motives to become involved in the voyage," she concluded. "Perhaps he shared the dream of many contemporaries that Columbus might find a kingdom of the Lost Tribes, a possible asylum for Jews far from the reaches of the Inquisition."

Whatever the motivation, the entire situation, according to the *I Ching,* changed into hexagram 61 Inner Truth. The judgment states:

Inner truth. Pigs and fishes.
Good fortune.
It furthers one to cross the great water.
Perseverance furthers.

This hexagram describes a situation in which external influence is lacking and an individual or community must rely wholly on itself—on inner truth. Pigs and fishes symbolize the least intelligent and most difficult and intractable people to influence.

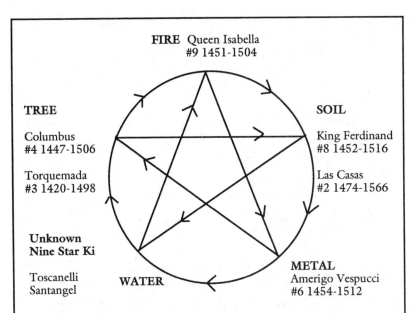

FIRE Queen Isabella
#9 1451-1504

TREE

Columbus
#4 1447-1506

Torquemada
#3 1420-1498

**Unknown
Nine Star Ki**

Toscanelli
Santangel

WATER

SOIL

King Ferdinand
#8 1452-1516

Las Casas
#2 1474-1566

**METAL**
Amerigo Vespucci
#6 1454-1512

Santangel was unable to prevent the Expulsion. However, he was able to convince the Queen to support Columbus' expedition and to finance the voyage. For this he turned to his fellow Jews and New Christians, including Medinaceli, Columbus' first patron in Spain; Abraham Senior, Crown Rabbi of Castile; and Isaac Abrabanel, a Jewish philosopher and principal tax collector. In addition to generous contributions of their own personal funds, they raised money for the voyage through the Hermandad, a brotherhood of police, local security guards, and tax-collectors which they controlled, by levying a special tax on butcher shops—another echo of "pigs and fishes."

Thus Europe's encounter with the New World was born in the crucible of religious persecution from the advent of Columbus' journey. He himself did not set a very good example, behaving at times more Catholic than the King and Queen and leaving a legacy of oppression and intolerance. But in the end, he came to regret his own zealotry and left a letter calling for the toleration of Christians, Jews, and Moors. Santangel's humanist motive to blunt the terror of the Inquisition and Columbus' final reflections—his moment of inner truth—must be added to the Pilgrims' colony in Massachusetts Bay, William Penn's Quaker colony in Pennsylvania, and other examples of religious dissent as primary spiritual influences shaping the American character and spirit. ❖

grown now in Spain as earlier it had grown in Italy or imported from the East—was whole, unrefined brown rice.

According to traditional Far Eastern medicine and philosophy, brown rice is the most biologically advanced of the cereal grains. Its regular consumption gives physical stamina and endurance, mental insight and flexibility, and a feeling of spiritual unity with others. Columbus exhibited all of these characteristics in seeing his remarkable project to fruition. Rice also creates more comprehensive, unified thinking. Where people eating meat and sugar see conflict and paradox, those eating grain and vegetables see the complementarity of opposites and unity. Columbus' idea of going west to reach the east is a brilliant, intuitive idea more akin to the philosophy of Lao Tzu and Bodhidharma than to Aristotle or Ptolmey. It conveys the sound of one hand clapping—or two directions clasping—that we associate with a paradoxical Zen koan. (Interestingly, Ryoanji, the famous Zen rock garden in Kyoto, and the Tea Ceremony were introduced in Japan during the very years Columbus was seeking backing for his voyage.) Also, Toscanelli, the Florentine astronomer and sage whose Oriental contacts, map, and letter may have inspired Columbus' quest, was a vegetarian with an ability to think in broad, dialectical terms. Toscanelli, the grandfather of the Americas, reminds us of an Eastern sage who heals a disease by treating its complementary opposite (e.g., strengthening the large intestine to cure the lungs).

During the First Voyage, rice and beans would have been staple food, so it is probable that Columbus continued to eat this well balanced and nourishing food through the first Encounter. Columbus' initial attitude toward the Tainos was gentle, peaceful, and respectful. He was constantly trying to protect them from being taken advantage of by his men. His objective, he noted, was to convert them "more by love than by force." Brown rice and other simple foods are particularly good for the digestive, circulatory, and nervous systems. They give the steadfast, even, calm energy necessary to pilot a ship through uncharted waters and to deal with frightened, hyperactive crewmen. They contribute to a heart and mind that is neither too expanded nor contracted—a steady outlook that is able to weather extremes of wind and water, fire and storm, passion and ice.

It is interesting how simple, macrobiotic-quality foods such as rice, chickpeas, and seaweed played a decisive role in Columbus' career. In another famous episode, on the return from his First Voyage, Columbus' caravel reached shore in Portugal and his crew were arrested. King John (who earlier had turned down Columbus' enterprise) summoned the navigator and tried to get him to disclose the route that he had sailed to the Indies. In an atmosphere charged with danger, Columbus cleverly showed the king the relative location of the lands he had discovered by having a native who accompanied him take a handful of beans and lay them out on the ground in the shape of the islands. But before a map could be drawn on paper, the beans were quickly scooped up. Against the advice of his counselors, the monarch did not kill Columbus but magnanimously let him depart home in recognition of his skill and bravery.

Columbus' simple diet would also help explain his ability to hold contradictory views, especially religious beliefs. In the Far East, it is common for people to identify themselves with two or more faiths. In China, for example, families traditionally celebrated Buddhist holidays, observed Taoist rituals, and patterned their daily life on a Confucian ethic. Similarly, in Japan today, many families celebrate a Shinto wedding, Christian holidays, and a Buddhist funeral. Eating grains and vegetables as their main food, they develop a flexible mind and see no conflict or contradiction in these spiritual practices. In the same way, many New Christians in Spain—eating a more plant-centered diet—were able to synthesize elements of Judaism and Christianity or practice both at the same time. The fierce, uncompromising ideology of the Inquisition required a hard, firm choice: either Christian or heretic, A or B, yes or no, we or they. The failure to see life as a complementary whole is the hallmark of modern dualism and the direct result of dietary extremes.

On the other side of the ledger, in Spain, as throughout Christiandom, many priests, monks, and religious ate very simply, observing the Church's prohibition of meat and animal food during Lent and other holy days. They often fasted, and penitential vows to abstain from food were common, among priest and laity. In a show of Christian faith, at the end of his First Voyage, a storm off the Iberian coast caused Columbus once again to have his men draw lots. The one who selected the marked pea vowed to fast on only bread and water the first Saturday after landfall. Again the lot fell to Columbus.

In contrast to special fasts such as this, some clerics carried asceticism to an extreme. Torquemada, the infamous Grand Inquisitor, slept on a hard board, wore a hair shirt, fasted for long periods of time, and abstained from meat. Bishop Jimenez de Cisnaros of Toledo, who served as confessor to the Queen, was also a devotee of bread and water and initiated a dietary reform of monasteries, forbidding rich foods, white flour, and fine wines. He later rose to the head of the Inquisition and, in vanquished Granada, oversaw the

73

burning of Moorish manuscripts preserving the Islamic literary heritage of 800 years, as well as forcing the Moors, like the Jews before them, to convert to Christianity or face death and exile.

Thus in all fairness, it must be acknowledged that some of the key inquisitors and proponents of state terror were extreme vegetarians. From the macrobiotic view, the clerics were too yang—contracted, tight, and inflexible—from fasting, from exposure to cold and other elements, from eating hard, dry bread, and other penances. Lacking soft whole grains and good quality beans, fresh vegetables, fruit, and other yin, they became more and more rigid and unyielding. (Lack of family life, including a gentle, loving wife and nice children, also creates a hard, yang outlook.) From the macrobiotic view, it is the overall balance of foods in the diet—not any one particular item such as meat, eggs, or rice—that governs our day to day health and happiness. From an energetic point of view, it appears that the main dietary imbalance contributing to the Inquisition was excessive consumption of poultry. The tribunal's scatterbrained, accusatory approach is typical, at a social level, of a society that has consumed too much chicken and eggs. People become overly suspicious (witness Chicken Little "the sky is falling"), as chicken fat contracts the pancreas and spleen, and like roosters and hens their minds become petty and critical. Superficial, nitpickey complaints were enough to send a victim to the stake—where bound and trussed up like a chicken on a spit, their limbs were sometimes torn off one by one before the pyres were lit.

After returning to Spain and being showered with honors and wealth, Columbus' attitude changed dramatically. He became more authoritarian and aggressive. This was partly the result of his meteoric rise to prominence and wealth. But as he grew rich and famous, he began to eat richer and more gourmet-style food. After his first audience with the monarchs, the Grand Cardinal of Spain, we learn, "took him to his house to dine with him, and bid him sit on the most preeminent seat, next to him, and had him served in a covered dish and his food tested first for poison, and that time was the first that his food was tested and served in a covered dish, and henceforward he was served with the solemnity and greatness required by his dignified title of Admiral."

From then on, as Las Casas makes clear in this passage, Columbus ate in a royal manner. We can be certain that the food set before his official taster did not include lowly brown rice or chickpeas.

By the time Columbus returned to the Caribbean the following year, his attitude toward the native people changed. In the Canaries,

74

he stocked up on hens, heifers, goats, ewes, and sows and returned as a colonizer and exploiter. In his defense, it can be argued that Columbus became more forceful only when he was provoked. On his return, he found La Navidad overrun and the thirty-nine Spanish sailors slain. (They had split into rival factions, seized native women, and generally created havoc until the Tainos killed them. Still, Columbus felt some punishment was necessary to restore order.) Also reports of fierce, cannibalistic tribes known as Caribs made a lasting impression on the Spanish and, in their mind, justified their harsh behavior. Anthropologists have dismissed these rumors as groundless, though there is some evidence that victorious Caribs, like warriors in some other traditional societies, ritually tasted or ate the livers of their defeated opponents. Columbus initially made a clear distinction between the gentle, peaceful Tainos and their hereditary enemies, the warlike Caribs, but ultimately even the Tainos were oppressed and enslaved. On his First Voyage, Columbus decried the mutinous act of his deputy, Pinzon, who sailed away looking for gold with the *Pinta* for two months without authorization as motivated by "greed and arrogance." On his Second Voyage, obsessed with obtaining wealth, Columbus himself demanded, upon penalty of death, that each male Taino over fourteen years of age— the same age that he set out to sea—supply a regular quota of gold. The Church's doctrine of just war allowed Christian armies to enslave enemies or rebels who rose up against them. This doctrine was used to justify slavery in the New World, though Ferdinand and Isabella opposed its introduction and repeatedly rebuked Columbus for his cruel treatment of the natives. In the dictatorial system organized by Columbus, we also see the influence of honey. In the Indies, he set himself up—in Isabella, the new capital—as Queen Bee and turned his own men and the native islanders into drones.

Extremes of rigidity and fantasy, inflexibility and illusion, lay at the root of this arrogance. The natives' nakedness was perceived as savagery, and in his journals Columbus, an otherwise keen observer, expresses wonder that the Indians have no religion, no agriculture, no culture. In fact, the Caribbeans had a sophisticated spiritual life, involving shamanistic practices and the ritual use of *zemis*, or icons that accumulated spiritual energy or power. They also had a way of farming, known as the *conuco* system, based on slash-and-burn agriculture that cleared forests, produced mineral-rich soil, and utilized mounds to grow yucca and a cornucopia of other crops. Columbus and generations of materially-oriented European colonizers simply could not see or appreciate these more subtle ways of life.

Both of these aspects of Native American culture are alive and well today, in the Caribbean and other parts of Central and South America, where they are increasingly recognized as an alternative approach to healing and farming. In a world beset by environmental destruction caused by the spread of modern civilization, including modern agriculture and modern medicine, traditional spiritual practices and traditional farming methods offer a holistic, comprehensive, ecologically balanced solution to personal and social ills.

Still, the Tainos and other native people bear some responsibility for their fate. They were not entirely innocent victims, citizens of a natural Utopia or Erewhon that was destroyed totally from without. Over generations, the Tainos had become too yin—too weak from the intake of excessive fruit, chocolate, and intoxicating beverages—to protect themselves from maurading Caribs. The Tainos particularly enjoyed snuff. Inhaling the crushed seeds of the piptadenia tree through a tube created hallucinations and enabled the Tainos to communicate with spirits. Ironically, Columbus may have left the Tainos in peace and sailed on toward the American mainland had he not noticed some ornaments of gold in the noses of several natives on the second day of his arrival. The nose, in traditional Oriental medicine and philosophy, corresponds with the heart. The use of ornamental nose rings, in the Caribbean, India, and elsewhere, can be seen as a way to strengthen the heart and circulatory system. Many customs, fashions, and trends like this have a physiological foundation. Weak hearts, including the will and strength to resist aggression, are caused by consuming too much fruit, spice, sweets, alcohol, and other extreme yin foods and beverages. The Tainos, like native people throughout the Americas, developed a more relaxed yin character and mind and were not able to counterbalance or neutralize their complementary opposite: the strong, yang European invaders. In contrast, a more centrally balanced culture, like the Vietnamese, eating primarily grains and vegetables, was able to offset waves of invaders and occupiers. Like the Jews, they were able to survive thousands of years of oppression and keep their dream alive because of adhering to a fundamentally centered way of eating, neither too yin or too yang. In our own era, the rise of nonviolence and the successful resistance of the Indian people to British rule and the triumph of the civil rights movement in America can be viewed as essentially a peaceful vegetarian or semi-macrobiotic response to oppression imposed by strong meat-eating cultures.

# Nine Star Ki:
# October 12, 1492

Columbus reached the New World on October 12, 1492. During that month, Nine Fire was in the middle, signifying a month of very active, dispersive energy. Nine Fire governs light, radiance, and glory and often brings active, explosive events. Meanwhile, Four Tree (Columbus' native sign) was in the Ninth House (the house of illumination), signifying that he was in the limelight this month.

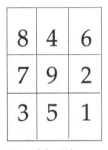

| 8 | 4 | 6 |
|---|---|---|
| 7 | 9 | 2 |
| 3 | 5 | 1 |

**Monthly Ki map for October, 1492**

Interestingly, in the Jewish calendar that year, October 12 fell on the seventh and last day of Sukkot, the traditional harvest festival known as Tabernacles. Known as Hosha-Na Rabbah, the days was customarily celebrated by Sephardic Jewish families with rejoicing, prayers, and a festive meal of *Dolma de Col Con Arros* (cabbage stuffed with rice), mixed vegetables, and stewed quinces. They also traditionally made seven circuits around the altar or Torah, carried cuttings of four plants symbolizing the four directions, and blew the *shofar*, or curved ram's horn. At the very moment the *Nina, Pinta,* and *Santa Maria* made landfall, exiled Spanish Jews were observing these spirallic festivals in scattered places throughout Europe, North Africa, and the Middle East. ❖

By the end of the Second Voyage, Columbus' health had sharply declined. The long weeks of fever, delirium, and pain in Hispaniola may have been enhanced by pineapple, an exotic tropical fruit that the explorer and his men discovered on this trip. Over the years, Columbus' arthritis worsened, especially in his feet, a condition he himself attributed to the cold and wind of the hazardous return from the First Voyage. This type of arthritis is linked to gout—the disorder traditionally caused by rich food intake. Pain in the big toe—the major symptom of gout—is associated in Oriental medicine with the liver and spleen meridians that end in that spot. In Oriental medicine, liver disorders are associated with anger and violence, and spleen disturbances give rise to envy, jealousy, and complaining. Such emotional displays typified Columbus' last years, and even to his friends and family he appeared a shell of his former self. In a forlorn appeal to the King and Queen, Columbus wrote: "I have wept for others so far; let Heaven have mercy now and let the earth weep for me." Some modern doctors have suggested that Columbus suffered from Reiter's syndrome, a tropical illness characterized by fever, diarrhea, inflammation of the joints, eyes, and urinary tract. Transmitted by the bacillus, *Shigella flexneri*, Reiter's syndrome was later common among Western armies in the tropics or sailors at sea. From the macrobiotic view, this disorder would also be primarily diet related. Intake of extreme yin and yang foods eventually create a weakening of the digestive system and an acidic internal environment in which potentially harmful microbes can thrive.

## Columbus' Last Bowl of Rice

 hich is the real Columbus: The sterling navigator or the cruel oppressor? The prophet of the New Jerusalem or the apostle of avarice? The faithful Christian or the clandestine Jew? While the evidence is compelling that Columbus was of Semitic heritage, we must remember that it is circumstantial. Indeed, until the end of his life, Columbus convinced himself that he was on the Asian mainland by selectively following geographical and linguistic clues that fit in with his own preconceived theory. For example, he confused Cubanacan, a region in the interior of Cuba where the natives reported gold, as the seat of the Great Khan. Other linguistic gaffes include mistaking Cybao (Haiti) for Cipangu (Japan).

Separating coincidence from conspiracy, and distinguishing the world of mundane reality from divine prophecy, are not always easy. Curiously, the Capitulations of Santa Fe, the famous document setting forth Columbus' demands to become Admiral and Viceroy of the Indies, was completed on April 30, 1492, the same day in which the final decree expelling the Jews was signed. Moreover, August 2, the deadline, fell on the ninth of Ab, the traditional date in the Jewish calendar in which the Jews were expelled from the First and Second Temple! These would appear to be coincidences—meaningful, perhaps Providential—but coincidences nonetheless. Thus we should take a lesson from Columbus' own life—an amazing mixture of truth and fantasy, coincidence and conspiracy—and keep an open mind about his true origin, motives, and religious sentiments. Even Salvatore de Madariaga, the originator of the theory of his Jewish origin, concludes: "Colón was neither Genoese nor Portuguese, nor Castilian, nor even Jewish. He was Cipanguish."

As Madariaga observes, Columbus was the prototype of Don Quixote, the knight from La Mancha with the pure intentions who lived in world of delusion. He was a latter-day prophet in a line stretching back to Moses, David, and Isaiah. He was the future Captain Nemo, hero of *Twenty Thousand Leagues Under the Sea*, and Captain Kirk on the voyage of the *Starship Enterprise*. He was living, if not entirely in another world, at least in multiple worlds. Ultimately, Columbus is a Zen koan, a paradoxical figure of conflicting identities, motives, and emotions, an undiscovered continent unto himself. On the one hand, he brought the two separate halves of the world together and inaugurated the process of making them whole. On the other, he left a bitter legacy of exploitation and enslavement that five centuries later has not entirely healed.

On his Third Voyage, Columbus was arrested in the Indies and returned home to Spain. None of his shocked men would put on the chains, and it was left for his own cook to do so. The cook put on the shackles, according to Las Casas, "with as saucy a front as if he were serving him new and precious dishes." The irony of this episode is Shakespearean. For abusing his health through improper eating, the Order of the Universe locked Columbus up, using his own cook as the instrument of supreme justice. On the way back to Spain, the once proud Admiral's diet no longer included covered dishes and a personal taster. It was undoubtedly rice and beans.

On returning to Spain, a penitent Columbus expressed the most noble sentiments of his life. In a letter to Queen Isabella and King Ferdinand, Columbus boldly called for religious toleration and harmony among all religions. "I say that the Holy Ghost works in Christians, Jews, and Moors and all men of any other sect and not merely in the learned, but in the ignorant." Proclaimed at the height of the Inquisition, this declaration was a breathtaking appeal. Stripped of his honors and wealth—made as naked as the inhabitants of the Indies—Columbus plunged into uncharted waters, listening to his own heartbeat one last time. He recognized that the Holy War against the infidel (Islam), the heretics (the Jews and unbelieving New Christians), and the unconverted (the Indians) to which he had lent his name and mission was a colossal lie. In the letter's composition and character, we can see Cristobal Colón, quill and paper before him, chewing one last bowl of rice and revealing his true mind before his Admiral's hat was returned and centuries of cruelty and prejudice—the bitter fruit of modern civilization—engulfed the New World. ❖

## Select Bibliography

Columbus, Christopher, *The Journal of Christopher Columbus*, translated by Cecil Jane, Bonanza, 1989.

Columbus, Christopher, *The Log of Christopher Columbus*, translated by Robert H. Fuson, International Marine Publishing Co., 1987.

Gerber, Jane S., *The Jews of Spain: A History of the Sephardic Experience*, The Free Press, 1992.

Litvinoff, Barnet, *1492: The Decline of Medievalism and the Rise of the Modern Age*, Avon Books, 1991.

Madariaga, Salvador de, *Christopher Columbus*, Fred Ungur, 1940, 1967.

Pohl, Frederick J., *Amerigo Vespucci, Pilot Major*, Octogon, 1966.

Rogozinski, Jan, *A Brief History of the Caribbean*, Meridian, 1992.

Rouse, Irving, *The Tainos: Rise and Decline of the People Who Greeted Columbus*, Yale University Press, 1992.

Rubin, Nancy, *Isabela of Castile: The First Renaissance Queen*, St. Martin's Press, 1992.

Tarducci, Francesco, *The Life of Christopher Columbus*, translated by Henry F. Brownson, H. F. Brownson, 1890.

West, Delno and August Kling, *The Libro de las profecias of Christopher Columbus*, University of Florida Press, 1991.

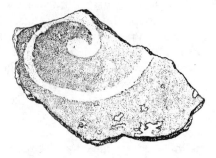

*Fragment of Taino pottery with a spiral motif.*

# William Shakespeare

*"A surfeit of the sweetest things*
*The deepest loathing to the stomach brings."*
                    —A Midsummer Night's Dream

*"With eager feeding food doth choke the feeder."*
                    —Richard II

*"Friends, you must eat no white bread . . . "*
                    —The Two Noble Kinsmen

*"I am a great eater of beef, and I believe that does harm to my wit."*
                    —Twelfth Night

*"So are you to my thoughts as food to life . . . "*
                    —Sonnet 75

*"It was a lover and his lass*
   *with a hey, and a ho, and hey-nanny-no,*
*That o'er the green cornfield did pass*
   *In the springtime, the only pretty ringtime.*
*When birds do sing, hey ding a ding, ding,*
   *Sweet lovers love the spring.*

*Between the acres of the rye,*
   *with a hey, and a ho, and hey-nanny-no,*
*These pretty country folks would be*
   *In the springtime, the only pretty ringtime.*
*When birds do sing, hey ding a ding, ding,*
   *Sweet lovers love the spring."*
                    —As You Like It

*So long as men can breathe or eyes can see,*
*So long* [macro] *lives this, and this gives life* [bios] *to thee."*
                    —Sonnet 18

---

*Overleaf: The Droeshout engraving published in the First Folio, 1623.*

# William Shakespeare
# Sweet Bodhisattva of Avon

he story of *Hamlet*—Shakespeare's greatest play and source of insight into his character and genius—is a tragic case history of psychologically induced heart disease. While the instrument of death in Act 5 is a thrust to the breast with the poisoned tip of a rapier, the sweet prince's noble heart is already sundered by the conflicting emotions within him. Just prior to the climactic swordplay, he confides to Horatio,

*Thou wouldst not think how ill all's here about*
*my heart . . .*

All the other protagonists in the play also die or suffer from pierced hearts. Polonius, Laertes, and Claudius die with sword thrusts to the breast. Ophelia is drowned trying to put out the dying embers of a broken heart. Gertrude, the Queen mother, succumbs to the poisoned cup, but her heart has already been "cleft in twain" by Hamlet, who has turned upon her for marrying Claudius so suddenly after her husband's death. Even Elder Hamlet, we learn from

*An early version of this essay appeared in* Diet for a Strong Heart *(with Michio Kushi, St. Martin's Press, 1985) in a chapter entitled "The Tragical Case History of Prince Hamlet."*

the Ghost, has died from a poison that has commingled with his blood and stopped his heart from beating. Madness, real and reigned, is a theme in the drama, but the disorders of the mind are subordinate to a more profound spiritual sickness in the human breast.

Throughout the play, we find internal evidence for some of the environmental and dietary factors that led to the tragic downfall of a prince, a royal family, and a state. Polonius, the platitudinous Lord Chamberlain, betrays a nutritional source for his superficial, incomplete, and overly refined observations:

> 'Tis too much prov'd, that with devotions visage
> And pious action we do sugar o'er
> The devil himself.

In the scene where Hamlet debates whether to slay his murderous uncle at prayer, he describes as "full of bread." By this he means that the usurping king is completely given over to sensory indulgence. We may be certain that it is not a reference to the wholesome dark bread of the Scandinavian countryside, but to the same rich "funeral bak'd meats [that] did coldly furnish forth the marriage tables" when Claudius and Gertrude married in unseemly haste after Elder Hamlet's death? Baked-meats were pies made of meat and spices and comprised a large part of the royal diet.

The Queen's dietary habits are not described, but it is probably safe to assume that she didn't do her own cooking. As a weak-willed mother and wife—"frailty, thy name is woman"—she evidently suffered from weak kidneys, probably brought about by too many sweets, fruits, and beverages. She also appears to have eaten too much dairy food. Her son describes her as "feed[ing]" on "this fair mountain" and "batten[ing] on this moor"—images that bring to mind a cow grazing. In admonishing her, Hamlet further exclaims that her "sense is apoplex'd." While this is metaphorical, high blood pressure and a propensity for stroke are indicated at the physical level.

Hamlet's "adder-ranged" friends, Rosencrantz and Guildenstern, attempt to betray him and "pluck out the heart of [his] mystery." Typically obsequious courtiers, they also had too yin a diet—undoubtedly too much Danish pastry. At one point, Hamlet compares them to nuts that an ape (the king, Claudius) keeps in the corner of his mouth.

Many of Hamlet's dietary allusions are, like this one, said

tongue in cheek. When Polonius says he will entertain the players "according to their desert," Hamlet quips, "Use every man after his desert, and who shall 'scape whipping?" However, Hamlet is profoundly aware of the central importance of food in human development. In the scene in which he discusses the art of playwrighting and acting with the players, he commends their performance as "an excellent play, well digested in the scenes." He goes on to approve of the lack of "sallets [salads] in the lines to make the matter savory" and compares the composition to more nourishing fare that is "as wholesome as [naturally] sweet." This passage is usually taken to embody Shakespeare's own philosophy of art and drama. The metaphor indicates that he disapproves of highly seasoned and spicy writing and novelty in acting. All the exotic side dishes of human experience may be found in Shakespeare's plays, but his clear, simple, direct style and language are grounded in durable whole cereal grains, clear sparkling water, and the salty wit of the earth. All else is excess. He is the consummate poet of tradition, balance, and common sense, taking timeless stories and truths and serving them up in a refreshing and original way.

In the scene where Claudius inquires about the fate of Polonius, Hamlet enlarges upon the theme of food as the evolutionary mode by which one species changes into another:

KING: *Now, Hamlet, where's Polonius?*
HAMLET: *At supper.*
KING: *At supper? Where?*
HAMLET: *Not where he eats, but where he is eaten. A certain convocation of politic worms are e'en at him. Your worm is your only emperor for diet ...*

This biological insight reminds us of the *Taittireeya Upanishad*:

*From food are born all creatures;*
*they live upon food, they are dissolved in food*
*Food is the chief of all things, the universal medicine ....*
*I am this world and I eat this world.*
*Who knows this, knows.*

There is an echo of this in three of Shakespeare's sonnets, including Sonnet 146:

*Shall worms, inheritors of this excess,*

> *Eat up thy charge? . . .*
> *Within be fed, without be rich no more.*
> *So shalt thou feed on Death, that feeds on men,*
> *And death once dead, there's no dying more.*

Indeed, the theme of the world stage being a vast compost pile permeates the Shakespearean canon. In *As You Like It*, Rosalind notes perceptively that men have died "and worms have eaten them, but not for love."

## Gentle Shepherd

 amlet is also well schooled in physiognomy and medical philosophy and is aware of his own heart rhythms. When he first sees the Ghost, he exclaims:

> *My fate cries out*
> *And makes each petty artire [artery] in*
>     *this body*
> *As hardy as the Nemean lions nerve.*

When the command to avenge his father's death is given, Hamlet swears vengeance with a reference to the heart.

> *Hold, hold, my heart,*
> *And you, my sinews, grow not instant old,*
> *But bear me stiffly up . . . .*

We learn from the Ghost that the murder took place in an orchard. This disclosure allows us to understand more fully Elder Hamlet's character and glimpse some of the underlying biological dynamics of the play. By all accounts, the Elder Hamlet was a strong, energetic monarch. His son compares his looks to Hyperion (the Sun), his eyes to Mars, and his brow to Jupiter. From this description, we may conclude that Elder Hamlet was very yang, and even as a Ghost his commanding presence is felt. The physical differences between Elder Hamlet and his brother, Claudius, are contrasted in the scene where Hamlet shows their pictures to his mother. In contrast to the noble features and bearing of the father, the physiognomy of the uncle is weak and ailing. He is referred to as ulcerous, corrupt, infected, "a mildew'd ear."

The source of Elder Hamlet's power and strength was evidently very yang food, including large amounts of meat pies, dried fish, and dairy food, as was customary in Scandinavia at that time as well as today. To balance this heavy animal food, the king was evidently in the habit of eating lighter, more relaxing fruits. Thus, he was napping in the orchard, probably after lunch, when Claudius attacked him. The Ghost's account of his death demonstrates an advanced awareness of his own cardiovascular system, as well as familiarity with dairy processing:

*That swift as quicksilver it [the poison] courses through*
*The natural gates and alleys of the body,*

*And with a sudden rigour it doth posset*
*And curd, like eager droppings into milk*
*The thin and wholesome blood . . . .*

The effect of the poison on the bloodstream was not unlike the atherosclerotic development of a thrombus, or blood clot, but in this case the process was rapidly speeded up, from many years to a few minutes.

Unlike his brother, Claudius was weak in temperament and resolve. He undoubtedly also ate too much meat and dairy products, but he did not counterbalance this with fruit, as did Elder Hamlet. Like many sedentary people, Claudius turned to alcohol. His drinking problem is alluded to throughout the play. Whenever possible he reaches for his "draught of Rhenish." These alcoholic binges repel Hamlet, who expresses disgust at his uncle's rouses and wassails and refers to him as "the bloat King." In the chapel scene, Hamlet forebears to slay him at prayer and vows to wait until Claudius is "drunk asleep, or in his rage." At prayer, meanwhile, the remorseful king makes oblique reference to his atherosclerotic will:

*Bow, stubborn knees; and heart with strings of steel,*
*Be soft as sinews of the new-born babe.*

To Elder Hamlet's extreme yang, Claudius represents extreme yin. Two brothers of the same stock, they mutually attract and repel each other. Just as meat and sugar are too volatile and explosive to coexist harmoniously within the human body on a regular basis, the two brothers collide, and their mutually exclusive ways of life lead to the degeneration of the body politic.

Hamlet's own constitution, personality, and way of eating is much more balanced and flexible than either his father's or uncle's. His "knotted locks" indicate that he inherited his father's curls, a sign of constitutional strength, but in his own words Hamlet' is "not Hercules." He is neither as muscular nor as energetic as his father. Hamlet's philosophical bent, scholarly vocation, and wry wit show a highly developed mental nature. However, by temperament he is not aloof, withdrawn, or otherwise excessively yin. He also was an accomplished fencer, dressed fashionably, looked forward to governing the state, and to Ophelia pressed his suit aggressively.

Hamlet's naturally balanced ("sweet") disposition, gentle wit, and well-developed mental and physical activities (like Shakespeare's) indicate that he ate primarily grains and vegetables. Of course, as the son of the king, he was brought up on the rich fare of the palace, but he did not indulge in the excesses of either his father or his uncle. As a student in Wittenberg, Hamlet apparently came to enjoy the dark bread of the medieval German countryside and other traditional fare that was more nourishing than what was available at home.

A good sign of all-around health is the condition of the liver, which is sensitive to extremes of meat, sugar, and alcohol. It is also the seat of anger, rage, and revenge. In a telling passage, Hamlet compares his own liver to a dove's, a bird proverbial for its gentleness:

> But I am pigeon-liver'd and lack gall
> To make oppression bitter . . . .

Hamlet's inaction—his lack of anger and will to carry out the revenge—is the dramatic theme of the play. It is the problem that has perplexed generations of viewers and critics and, in T. S. Eliot's words, made *Hamlet* "the 'Mona Lisa' of literature." Why does Hamlet procrastinate in avenging his father's death? Why does he not immediately carry out the vow he has made to the Ghost? Why does he compel the poor spirit to return from the dead to his mother's chamber "to whet thy almost blunted purpose"? What is he waiting for?

The answer, of course, is very simple. Hamlet is constitutionally unable to slay another human being, even in retaliation for horrendous crimes. He has eaten grains and vegetables for most of his life and, by nature, has become very peaceful and forgiving. He recognizes that vengeance is just, but he also understands that there is a higher law. He abhors the prevalent code of "an eye for an eye." Moreover, he sees that a potential for excess and imbalance is in us all and that he will inevitably become corrupted by taking up arms. The Viking code of vengeance is anathema to him and he instinctively rejects it, along with the predatory way of life and way of eating from which it springs. Thus is set in motion an age-old dilemma: Should he observe ties of blood and loyalty or follow the promptings of his own heart?

In portraying Hamlet, Shakespeare would appear to be at his most autobiographical. Throughout the plays, he displays a tenderness, mercy, and compassion that is the antithesis of the Elizabethan courtier, hero, and emblem of manhood. He sympathizes with slain deer, he recoils at blood sports and butchering, he softens or edits out entirely the bloodshed and violence from many of his historical and literary sources, and he embraces suffering humanity with all of its faults and frailties. "But kindness, nobler ever than revenge," Orlando's inclination in *As You Like It*, could also be his creator's.

After initially promising to obey the Ghost's command, Hamlet discovers that he is constitutionally and temperamentally unsuited to carry it out. Moreover, on further reflection, he wonders whether the Ghost is really "a spirit of health or goblin damn'd" leading him on to folly? Hamlet must have proof that Claudius is really guilty. Thus he devises the play within a play to force his uncle's hand by recreating the murder scene. As the drama unfolds, Hamlet meditates on the relation of head and heart:

> . . . . *Blest are those*
> *Whose blood and judgment are so well commeddled*
> *That they are not a pipe for Fortune's finger*
> *To sound what stop she please. Give me that man*
> *That is not passion's slave, and I will wear him*
> *In my heart's core, ay, in my heart of heart.*

The struggle within Hamlet's breast between reason and passion, god and beast, nobility and baseness, forgiveness and revenge, and other pairs of complementary and antagonistic qualities is the universal field of experience on which we all contend. Even as he steels himself for the deed, Hamlet prays that he will not be corrupted by his act:

> . . . *Now could I drink hot blood,*
> *And do such bitter business as the day*

*Would quake to look on. Soft, now to my mother.*
*O heart lose not thy nature. Let not ever*
*The soul of Nero [Claudius] enter this firm bosom;*
*Let me be cruel, not unnatural.*

Hamlet understands the laws of opposites and recognizes that good and evil are inextricably bound to each other. The human condition embraces all dualities, and freedom is found not in violent conquest or subduing, but in balancing, harmonizing, and unifying. Yet in the end, as he fears all along, Hamlet becomes what he is fighting against. In a rash moment, during a highly emotional meeting with the Queen, he stabs the eavesdropper behind the arras, whom he takes to be Claudius, and finds instead that he has slain Polonius. In doing so, Hamlet kills another son's father and becomes the object of Laertes' revenge. To Horatio, Hamlet confesses:

*For by the image of my cause I see*
*The portraiture of his [Laertes']. . .*

Just as Claudius dies by the same poisoned cup that he has prepared for another, the prick to Hamlet's breast with the tainted rapier represents the seed of imbalance that exists within the most noble heart.

Although Hamlet is initially in good physical and mental shape, the shock of the Ghost's revelation about his uncle and mother severely tries his balanced constitution and harmonious temperament. Like everyone else, Hamlet has physical strengths and weaknesses. In his case the heart is especially well developed, and he is able to endure enormous pressure and stress, avoiding extremes of both rashness of action and a paralyzed will. However, Hamlet's weakest organ is the lungs, and the play describes the progressive deterioration of its functions.

There are many references to Hamlet's worsening lung condition. His own coloring and thoughts are consistently described as pale, the hue associated with lung deficiencies in both traditional Western and Oriental medicine. For example, when the King and Queen ask what troubles him after he has seen the Ghost, he cites as one of the trappings of his woes the "windy suspiration of forc'd breath." Later, he observes in himself:

*And thus the native hue of resolution [blood red]*
*Is sicklied o'er with the pale cast of thought . . .*

Hamlet engages in special exercises to strengthen his lungs:

> . . . *If it please his*
> *Majesty, it is the breathing time of day with me.*

During the climactic dual with Laertes, his mother describes him as "scant of breath."

These and other references to Hamlet's pale countenance and breathing trouble are traditional symptoms of melancholy, the sickness associated with the lungs. In traditional Western philosophy and medicine, stretching back to Hippocrates and Galen, the four humors (*see diagram*) were conceived of as fluids or vital energies that circulated in the body. The humors were also influenced by environmental factors, such as wind, water, temperature, and direction. A person's physical and mental attributes were believed to depend upon the given balance of humors in the body. For example, Hamlet says,

> *I am but mad north-north-west. When the wind is southerly, I know a*
> *hawk from a handsaw.*

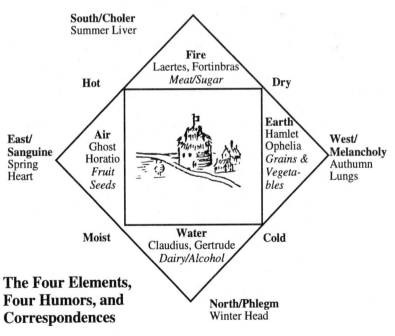

South/Choler
Summer Liver

Fire
Laertes, Fortinbras
*Meat/Sugar*

Hot     Dry

East/
Sanguine
Spring
Heart

Air
Ghost
Horatio
*Fruit
Seeds*

Earth
Hamlet
Ophelia
*Grains &
Vegeta-
bles*

West/
Melancholy
Authumn
Lungs

Moist     Cold

Water
Claudius, Gertrude
*Dairy/Alcohol*

**The Four Elements,
Four Humors, and
Correspondences**

North/Phlegm
Winter Head

This is a direct allusion to traditional humoral philosophy as expressed in Timothy Bright's *A Treatise of Melancholy*, published in 1586, in which therapeutic breathing is recommended for weakened lungs and the melancholy humor. "The air meet for melancholic folk ought to be . . . open and patent to all wind . . . especially to the south and south-east." Each of the four winds rules a particular malady and can be counterbalanced by the complementary opposite force. Melancholy was believed to arise in the spleen from an excess of black bile, weakening the lungs and heart and producing chronic sadness and sorrow.

In addition to melancholy, there were three other humors. A choleric person was said to have yellow bile as the chief humor and to be governed by the liver. This humor produced an active, fiery personality and in excess led to the person's being bad-tempered and easily angered. Laertes is of this type. A phlegmatic person, demonstrating a more calm and self-possessed temperament, was ruled by the phlegm, or thick mucus in the body. Excessive phlegm rapidly led to sluggishness. Gertrude was essentially phlegmatic, as was Claudius, though he also exhibited strong choler. A sanguine individual, under the sovereignty of the heart and the blood, presented a cheerful and optimistic countenance. Horatio is a good example of this type.

The doctrine of humors generally corresponds to the Far Eastern cycle of the five transformations (*see Appendix*), which can be viewed as four cardinal energies encircling one central energy. From at least the sixth century B.C. until the seventeenth century A.D., when modern science arose and began to sever the connection between mind and body, this way of thinking prevailed in the West. The doctrine of humors formed the philosophical foundation of Elizabethan drama, and, like physiognomy, references to it permeate Shakespeare's plays and poems. In *The Tempest*, for example, Ariel is said to be composed of fire and air, while Caliban is made of earth and water. In Sonnet 44, Shakespeare laments his own Caliban-like dullness:

> *But that, so much of earth and water wrought,*
> *I must attend time's leisure with my moan,*
> *Receiving naught by elements so slow*
> *But heavy tears, badges of either's woe.*

In Sonnet 45, he continues the image and, like Hamlet, sinks into despondency:

*The other two, slight air and purging fire,*
*Are both with thee, wherever I abide;*
*The first my thought, the other my desire,*
*These present-absent with swift motion slide.*
*For when these quicker elements are gone*
*In tender embassy of love to thee,*
*My life, being made of four, with two alone*
*Sinks down to death, oppressed with melancholy.*

In *Hamlet,* just prior to the first visitation of his father's ghost, Hamlet philosophizes,

*By their o'ergrowth of some complexion*
*Oft breaking down the pales and forts of reason . . .*

Complexion is a special term referring to the humors. It is defined by the *Oxford English Dictionary*: "In the physiology and natural philosophy of the Middle Ages: the combination of supposed qualities (cold or hot, and moist or dry) in a certain proportion, determining the nature of a body, plant, etc.; the combination of the four 'humours' of the body in a certain proportion, or the bodily habit attributed to such combination; 'temperament.'"

Following the play-within-a-play scene, in which he unmasks his uncle as his father's murderer, Hamlet and Guildenstern exchange observations following Claudius's angry departure,

GUILDENSTERN: *The King, sir—*
HAMLET: *Ay, sir, what of him?*
GUILDENSTERN: *Is in his retirement marvellous*
*distempered.*
HAMLET: *With drink, sir?*
GUILDENSTERN: *No, my lord, with choler.*
HAMLET: *Your wisdom should show itself more richer to signify this to the doctor, for for me to put him to his purgation would perhaps plunge him into more choler.*

There are many other references in the play to the four humors, and also to the four elements—earth, air, water, fire. One of the play's most famous passages,

*O that this too too sullied flesh would melt,*
*Thaw and resolve itself into a dew . . .*

refers to the traditional remedy for melancholy. A cold, dry humor associated with congealing of the blood, melancholy was believed to result from an excess of the earth element to which it corresponded. To relieve this overabundance, earth was melted into water, which in turn resolved itself into a dew. Dew was also considered one of the secondary humors in medieval medicine.

These examples are meant to illustrate the traditional world view, which Shakespeare shared. The play as a whole, including the characters and complex motives of the protagonists, cannot really be understood without knowledge of the doctrine of the four humors. Similarly Ophelia's distribution of flowers to the King and Queen and her brother requires a familiarity with herbalism. When she gives Laertes rosemary, symbolic of remembrance, he is motivated to avenge the death of their father, Polonius, and thus Ophelia unwittingly serves the same function with respect to her brother as the Ghost does with respect to Hamlet. All these allusions, taken for granted by the Elizabethan mind, are usually lost on the modern reader.

Given a predisposition to weak lungs, it is not surprising that Hamlet chose to put on an "antic disposition" characteristic of certain forms of melancholy. Had he been choleric by nature, he might have chosen to conceal his method behind a mask of drunkenness. If phlegmatic, he might have withdrawn into a catatonic stupor or if overly sanguine, feigned epilepsy.

Much of Hamlet's paleness and breathing trouble can be laid to the shock of his father's murder and his mother's over-hasty remarriage. His heart is overburdened by the truth he has discovered and the demands expected of him. A strained heart, as we see in Oriental medicine and humoral doctrine, directly afflicts the lungs. However, dietary influences also played an important role. During the course of his madness, Hamlet forgoes meals and eats erratically. The action in the play spans four months, the exact time it takes for the quality of the red blood cells to change. While he was in excellent condition at the start of the play, neglect of diet over a period of 120 days would have completely transformed his blood quality, affecting the quality of his thoughts and feelings as well as his stamina and energy.

During this time, Hamlet's attitude toward life changes fundamentally and he becomes despondent and suicidal. The world that formerly held so much promise for him becomes stifling and unbearable.

*. . . What piece of work is a man, how noble in reason, how infinite in faculties, in form and moving how express and admirable, in action how like an angel, in apprehension how like a god: the beauty of the world, the paragon of animals—and yet, to me, what is this quintessence of dust?*

This pessimistic observation reflects underlying lung troubles, and Hamlet complains more and more about the poor quality of the air. In the same speech he declares:

*. . . This brave o'erhanging firmament, this majestical roof fretted with golden fire, why, it appeareth nothing to be but a foul and pestilent congregation of vapours.*

He laments fate, which

*Tweaks me by the nose, gives me the lie i'th' throat*
*As deep as to the lungs . . .*

The suffocation that he feels in his chest is projected onto the world, and he observes "Denmark's a prison."

The humors were produced primarily by the type of food a person ate, and an imbalanced diet would lead to either an excess or deficiency and resultant physical, mental, or spiritual disorders. In an essay on *Melancholy* translated into English in 1594, near the time *Hamlet* was written, Peter de la Primaudaye, a member of the French Academy, defined humor as "a liquid and running body into which food is converted in the liver, to this end: that bodies might be nourished and preserved by them."

Hamlet's worsening state of health, brought about by the shocking disclosures and an irregular way of eating, culminates in his cruelty to Ophelia. As his blood quality deteriorates, he becomes more suspicious, defensive, and withdrawn—true melancholic characteristics—and treats his friends as enemies. As his lungs decline, his kidneys—the seat of will—begin to suffer, and his resolve weakens.

At sea, on the voyage to England, Hamlet undergoes a major transformation. Irresolution and vacillation give way to resolve and new energy. Part of this change in behavior can be attributed to the change of environment and a more wholesome and regular diet. Aboard ship, spicy baked-meats, dairy food, Danish pastries, and other freshly prepared foods that were extremely imbalanced were not available. Instead, the shipboard regimen probably consisted primarily of dried salted fish, seafood, and whole grain biscuits and crackers. From his newly returned resolve, we also see that Hamlet's kidneys are functioning better, possibly as the result of some mineral-rich seaweed in his ocean-bound diet. As a result of this more yang fare, Hamlet returns to his senses, and his intuition begins to function again. Fortuitously, he discovers that the commission carried by Rosencrantz and Guildenstern from Claudius instructs the English court to put him to death.

From this point on, Hamlet acts every bit the true heir to the Danish throne. He jumps ship when the pirates attack in a display of nimble physical dexterity. Back in Denmark once again, he sends a bold letter to Claudius, defies Laertes, jumps in the open grave, declares his eternal love for Ophelia, and in the tragic finale makes up for his vacillation by making Claudius drink from the poisoned cup after stabbing him through the breast. As he lies dying from his own wounds, Hamlet turns to Horatio and implores,

> *If thou didst ever hold me in thy heart,*
> *Absent thee from felicity awhile,*
> *And in this harsh world draw thy breath in pain*
> *To tell my story.*

Projected onto his only true friend in the world, Hamlet's last words, referring to the heart and lungs, echo the physical and psychological imbalance that has beset him. Horatio's response,

> *Now cracks a noble heart. Good night, sweet prince,*
> *And flights of angels sing thee to thy rest.*

underscores the heart image that is the play's guiding metaphor.

## The Incensed Points of Mighty Opposites

t the social level, the contest between Hamlet and Claudius can be viewed as the conflict between traditional and modern society. According to two scholars in *Hamlet's Mill: An Essay Investigating the Origins of Human Knowledge and Its Transmission through Myth,* Shakespeare's play derives from an early

Scandinavian myth portraying the precession of the equinoxes, or the change in world epochs. The original Ameleth is the custodian of a great mill (the stars revolving around the North Pole), which turns out peace and plenty until decay and chaos set in. *Ameleth*, Hamlet's original name, derives from the same root word of ambrosia and nourishment and means "the grain." His uncle is said to represent "the grinding" or maelstrom force.

Whatever the exact mythological origins, Hamlet—like Mona Lisa—is the distillation of well-developed human culture. He has a deep sympathy for the natural world and in his life exhibits the qualities of moderation, balance, and harmony associated with health and vitality. Claudius is the embodiment of excess, novelty, overstimulation, and cleverness. In the King's person we find the seeds of the modern scientific mentality. Debating about how to rid himself of his nephew, Claudius reflects,

> *. . . Diseases desperate grown*
> *By desperate appliance are reliev'd,*
> *Or not at all.*

Deciding to send Hamlet to his death, the King soliloquizes, extending the medical metaphor,

> *. . . Do it, England;*
> *For like the hectic in my blood he rages,*
> *And thou must cure me . . . .*

Again, when his plans are thwarted and Hamlet returns, Claudius convinces Laertes to challenge him to a duel with an image of sickness and disease:

> *. . . But to the quick of th'ulcer:*
> *Hamlet comes back . . .*

Modern society, rather than reflecting on the internal origin of its private and public ills, seeks an external cause to be rooted out and destroyed. The two methods that Claudius uses—poisonous drugs and the knife blade—are the methods of modern warfare and the operating room.

In contrast, Hamlet, the very incarnation of the self-reflective soul, is always looking within himself for the source of his troubles and is ever mindful of becoming what he is fighting against. "Taint not thy mind," his father's Ghost—the voice of ancestral tradition—warns him. While Hamlet also adopts some of the imagery of disease to refer to his uncle, he tries not to adopt his methods. These two ways of viewing the world are the real combatants on the stage. In describing to Horatio the fates of Rosencrantz and Guildenstern, Hamlet remarks,

> 'Tis dangerous when the baser nature comes
> Between the pass and fell incensed points
> Of mighty opposites.

It is this inner battle raging between reason and appetite, forgiveness and revenge, moderation and intemperance, and order and chaos that the outer struggle mirrors. Just before taking up swords with Laertes at the end, Hamlet confesses to Horatio,

> . . . in my heart there was a kind of fighting
> That would not let me sleep. . . .

## Let Be

he Elizabethan society for which this play was performed stood on the threshold of the modern age. Shakespeare saw clearly the approaching philosophy that would separate mind and body and reduce life to mechanistic functioning. Claudius embodies this mechanistic spirit: the impulse to uproot nature without considering the consequences and to use others as instruments to our own ends. This way of thinking is what is rotten in Denmark—and the entire modern world.

Hamlet represents traditional society that dies to make way for the new and whose spirit will live on when technique, novelty, and excess have run their course. Such is the order of things. As "night follows day," yin follows yang and yang succeeds yin. A period of artistic culture, spiritual development, and peace gives way to an era of technological progress, material development, and conflict. For all of its heavenly denizens and allusions to the occult, *Hamlet* like Shakespeare's other plays makes clear that the evils of this world come not without from ghosts or demons, but from within ourselves. In *Hamlet*, meat and sugar (symbolized by the final triumph of Fortinbras, another choleric type) replace grains and vegetables. And so the spiral unfolds, each turn resulting in a slightly different expression of the cycle and leading eventually to a higher synthesis. This is the order of the universe—the alternation of yin and yang, of Carnival and Lent, of comedy and tragedy.

In *Hamlet*, Shakespeare, the poet laureate of traditional society, poses the basic dilemma of the modern age: How to live in and transform a world that appears "weary, stale, flat, and unprofitable." All about Hamlet is death and disorder, corruption and degeneration. It is interesting that Shakespeare chose an ancient Danish legend as the vehicle for this purpose. However remote and medieval the setting, the Scandinavian environment is surprisingly modern regarding nutrition. The Viking diet—heavy animal food, dairy products, sweetmeats, and alcohol—has pretty much conquered the modern world. Today the world's highest consumption of fat and cholesterol—and the highest rate of heart disease—are still found in regions of Scandinavia.

Hamlet's aversion to the atmosphere of meat and alcohol is a recurrent theme. He abhors the effects of Claudius's drinking parties on the common wealth and health:

> *This heavy-headed revel east and west*
> *Makes us traduc'd and tax'd of other nations—*
>
> *They clepe us drunkards, and with swinish phrase*
> *Soil our addition. . .*

He upbraids his mother's faithless conduct,

> *Nay, but to live*
> *In the rank sweat of an enseamed bed,*
> *Stew'd in corruption . . .*

The image is drawn from seam, a type of saturated animal fat used in cooking and making stews. The metaphor is carried further when he tells her in a subsequent passage,

> *. . . Forgive me this my virtue;*
> *For in the fatness of these pursy times*
> *Virtue itself of vice must pardon beg. . .*

The word *pursy*, meaning flabby or puffed up, reinforces the image.

As a commentary on contemporary English excess, *Hamlet* had a curious parallel. King James, during whose early reign the play was believed to have been written, once gave a banquet at which the honored guest, King Christian of Denmark, collapsed at dinner; Anne, his daughter, Queen of England, passed out on the dance floor; three court ladies were too drunk to participate in a court masque; and another royal favorite spilled a rich custard all over the King.

Despite the violent, oppressive environment of the court, Hamlet learns to come to terms with existence. At the close, he no longer curses that "the world is out of joint" but accepts his obligation to set it right and restore harmony. He no longer views the world in the dualistic terms of "to be or not to be" but, embracing the evil along with the good, says "the readiness is all . . . Let be." He no longer rejects death and disorder as chaotic and random but finds "a special providence in the fall of a sparrow." As his own physical strength and vitality return, Hamlet's faith in the meaning of life is renewed, and he accepts his own tragic part in the universal drama,

*There's a divinity that shapes our ends, Rough-hew them how we will.*

Hamlet's heart is at peace at last.

Such, in brief, is the philosophical foundation to Shakespeare's play. The many levels to Hamlet spring from a deep understanding of nature and the order of the universe, including the art of physiognomy and the doctrine of the four elements. In the same way that

*. . . Heaven's face does glow*
*O'er this solidity and compound mass [the Earth's four*
*elements]. . .*

so Shakespeare looks upon human nature as conditioned by the four humors. Each of his characters, as we have seen, embodies traditional qualities, eats specific foods, and suffers from specific illnesses associated with one of these vital energies.

Although this harmonious and orderly way of looking at life has disappeared and the modern world draws its breath in pain, Hamlet remains to tell the story under the starlit sky until whole grains (the staff of life), native common sense, and felicity return.

# Laureate of the Human Heart

Shakespeare expresses the eternal order of the universe in a near-perfect unity of form and content. Each line of his plays contains five pairs of syllables. The first is unaccented, the second accented, and so on. This pattern of alternating stresses imitates the human heartbeat, the rhythmic expansion of diastole and contraction of systole. When recited out loud, iambic pentameter closely parallels the actual rate of the beating heart. The normal heart beats about 65 to 70 times a minute. We can recite about 14 lines of iambic pentameter a minute—or 70 syllables. For example, when his mother accuses him of madness, Hamlet replies in a way that perfectly unifies form and contect: *"My pulse as yours doth temperately keep time/And makes as healthful music . . . . "* This is a key to his universal appeal.     ❖

## Good Night, Sweet Prince

 amlet's dilemma—finding meaning and taking action to redeem a degenerate world—invites comparison with that of two other princes in world literature, Arjuna and Siddhartha. Like Hamlet, Arjuna, the hero of the *Bhagavad Gita*, is called upon to revenge the wrong done his household and finds himself facing mortal combat with his uncles, cousins, and other relations. Sinking down in his chariot on the battlefield, Arjuna casts away his weapons and refuses to fight. His charioteer, Krishna, then proceeds to enlighten him about the nature of reality and the laws of cause and effect, and like the Ghost of Elder Hamlet spurs him to recover his resolve. Like Hamlet, Siddhartha, the future Buddha, is put off by the suffering, sorrow, ugliness, and brutality around him. The palace is dreary and insufferable and he finds he can no longer live in its midst.

In modern medical terms, all three princes face the spiritual "fight or flight" syndrome. Hamlet and Arjuna choose to stand their ground and accept their destiny. Siddhartha chooses to leave the royal estates and seek harmony in another environment. After trying out various extreme practices, Siddhartha settles under a tree to meditate on the sorrows of the human heart. There he eats brown rice and seeks to unify his mind with the infinite. After a long period of self-reflection, Siddhartha attains enlightenment. As the Buddha, the Awakened One, he goes on to devote his life to teaching a middle way between extremes of yin and yang and a philosophy grounded in compassion, serving others, forgiveness, endless gratitude, and a simple way of eating. As the *New York Times* art critic observed in a recent review of a Buddhist art exhibit, "In all these sculptures and paintings we see the Asian equivalent of a Prince Hamlet who took the right turning."

Hamlet was relatively enlightened, and in the end he and Laertes forgave each other. However, he was not able to reconcile all the opposites within himself. Had he been more "fair, kind, and true"—as Shakespeare described his own ideal in the Sonnets—and had he been able to see all phenomena as complementary and antagonistic, Hamlet would have initially pacified the spirit of his father's Ghost, pointing out that the seeds of his murder lay in his own past misdeeds, and prayed for the smooth journey of his soul to the next world. As a *bodhisattva*, or Buddha in training, he would have forgiven Claudius and Gertrude. He would not have turned against Ophelia but married her and, if the King and Queen couldn't be changed, set off with her for Vinland. There, in a new Arcadia, they could have enjoyed a new life together, sowing the fields, rearing a family, and singing "the merry songs of peace" we associate with Shakespeare's comedies. If the court at Elsinore had observed a more natural way of life, including a more centrally balanced diet, the "carnal, bloody, and unnatural acts" might have been averted and "purposes mistook" might not have "fall'n on th'inventors' heads."

For modern society today, poised between "the pass and fell incensed points of mighty opposites"—such as cancer and heart disease, nuclear war and terrorism, and great wealth and abject poverty—there is still time to transmute tragedy into comedy and create a happy ending.                                                                    ❖

## Select Bibliography

Giorgio de Santillana and Hertha von Dechend, *Hamlet's Mill*, David Godine, 1977.

Russell, John, "The Image of the Buddha Continues to Enthrall," *New York Times*, December 2, 1984.

Shakespeare, William, *Hamlet*, the Arden Shakespeare, edited by Harold Jenkins, Methuen, 1982.

# Christopher Marlowe

*"Let me peruse this face."*
                    —Romeo and Juliet

*"O, what art of physiognomie might one behold."*
                    —Shakespeare, The Rape of Lucretia

*"Come with me and be my love*
*and we will all the pleasures prove . . . "*
                    —Marlowe, The Passionate Pilgrim

*"Our souls whose faculties can comprehend*
*The wondrous architecture of the world,*
*And measure every wandering planet's course,*
*Still climbing after knowledge infinite,*
*And always moving as the restless spheres,*
*Wills us to wear ourselves and never rest . . . "*
                    —Marlowe, Tamburlaine

*"If Shakespeare is the dazzling sun of this mighty period,*
*Marlowe is certainly the morning star."*
                    —Alfred Lord Tennyson

*"Marlowe is the greatest discoverer, the most daring pioneer, in all our*
*poetic literature. Before Marlowe there was no genuine blank verse and gen-*
*uine tragedy in our language. After his arrival the way was prepared, the*
*path made straight for Shakespeare."*
                    —A. C. Swinburne

*". . . my life in darkenes cast."*
                    —Mary Sidney, Psalms

SILVIUS:  *My gentle Phoebe bid me give you this:*
                *I know not the contents; but, as I guess*
                *By the stern brow and waspish action . . .*
                *It bears an angry tenor . . .*

ROSALIND:  *. . . Were man as rare as phoenix.*
                    —As You Like It

---

*Overleaf: Portrait believed to be that of Christopher Marlowe, Corpus*
*Christi College, Cambridge, 1585.*

## Christopher Marlowe
# The True Shakespeare

hose who doubted that Shakespeare wrote the works attributed to him comprise a literary galaxy of the highest magnitude: Nathaniel Hawthorne, Ralph Waldo Emerson, Walt Whitman, Oliver Wendell Homes, John Greenleaf Whittier, Sigmund Freud, and Henry James. The main argument against William Shakespeare being the real author of the plays and poems published in his name is that he came from a rural household, had only a rudimentary education, and lacked the refinement to depict the English Court and aristocratic life that form the backdrop to the plays. From the macrobiotic perspective, Shakespeare's country roots and basic education constitute his greatest asset. Eating simply, following the rhythms of nature, and developing into a keen observer and shrewd judge of the human heart, he blossomed into the supreme poet of the English language. By contrast, the other claimants to the authorship—assorted earls, lords, and other members of the Court—were highly bred and overeducated. For the most part, too arrogant or foppish, they lacked the biological foundation and universal sympathy to have penned the plays.

Who was Shakespeare? What did he look like? And what do his features tell us? The famous engraving in the First Folio that prefaces the first collected edition of the Bard's works in 1623 carries the enigmatic inscription:

*To the Reader.*
*This Figure, that thou here seest put,*
*It was for gentle Shakespeare cut;*
*Wherein the Grauer had a strife*

*with Nature, to out-doo the life:*
*O, could he but haue drawne his wit*
*As well in brasse, as he hath hit*
*His face; the Print would then surpasse*
*All, that was euer writ in brasse.*
*But, since he cannot, Reader, looke*
*Not on his Picture, but his Booke.*

Martin Droeshout, the engraver, was only fifteen when Shakespeare died in 1616. Shakespeare lived to age fifty-two, so the portrait showing a younger man in his late thirties or early forties—about the age when he wrote the late plays—could not have been drawn from life. Whether it was based on an earlier portrait is not known. Our modern image of Shakespeare, derived exclusively from this engraving, depicts a balding middle-aged man, with moderately long hair and thin moustache attired in a fashionable Elizabethan doublet and stiff collar. The eyes are level, fixed, and penetrating, and there is a hint of a pout on his mouth. The overall impression is one of focus and concentration, balance and constancy. The high dome corresponding to a well developed nervous system (and highly charged mid-brain) betokens a supremely gifted mind, but the ill-fitting formal attire suggests an intellect that is anxious to slip free from social conventions and the constricting framework of religious and political authority. Beneath the serenity, there is a bittersweet aura, like the ending to many of his plays.

The structure of the head—in between oval and oblong in shape—suggests that Shakespeare's parents and ancestors ate plenty of whole grains and vegetable-quality food. (Note how remarkably the head itself is shaped like a kernel of grain, a bean, or a squash.) The eyebrows are thick, even, and slightly curving down, showing vitality, steadiness, and a gentle nature. The strong nose and well-developed nostrils also show reservoirs of constitutional strength and perseverance as well as strong nervous, circulatory, and respiratory functions. While we cannot see Shakespeare's ears, the partially visible left earlobe further suggests that his mother ate plenty of nourishing staple foods. Combined with the predominantly vertical orientation to the face, the alert almond eyes confirm a more artistic, yin nature. The wide-set brows, another yin characteristic, indicate a tendency toward loss and separation, especially lost love.

Shakespeare's face is almost perfectly balanced and symmetrical—like his plays—and from the angle of the portrait it is hard to determine whether the right or left side—showing the influence of the mother and father—is more dominant. Curiously, his left eye is lower than his right, reminiscent of the "one auspicious and one dropping eye" in *Hamlet*. However, this may be because the whole engraving is printed askew, not because young Droeshout executed a budding Cubist perspective. The tight corners of the inside right eye and the outside left eye show the predominant influence of Shakespeare's maternal grandmother and paternal grandfather respectively.

According to oral tradition, Shakespeare had red or auburn hair, which is a sign of yang constitutional vitality. The mouth and lips are well-formed, neither too contracted or expanded. However, the puffiness of the lower lip, especially on his right side, suggests that Shakespeare's intestines were slightly expanded at the time of the drawing, probably from too much salad, sweets, and wine. The most conspicuous conditional feature, the bags under his eyes, show a weakening kidney condition, brought on by too much yin. Balding in the front of the head is also caused by excessive yin—especially fruit, sweets, and alcohol—so that together these signs indicate that by middle age Shakespeare was beginning to experience the effects of mild dietary imbalance.

The other principal likeness of Shakespeare is the Chandos portrait, which bears a resemblance to the Droeshout engraving. It may have been composed by Richard Burbage, a colleague of Shakespeare who was both an actor and painter. However, its authenticity is suspect and historians generally have not accepted it. Nevertheless, for diagnostic purposes, it confirms the conclusions we have drawn from the Droeshout engraving. The Chandos portrait shows a slightly younger, more romantic

*Left*, the present bust of Shakespeare in Stratford dating to 1748. *Right*, the original bust of Shakespeare, according to a copy published in 1656.

figure, with a fuller beard, broader moustache, and frizzier hair. Unlike the rather bloodless expression in the engraving, the poet looks at us with more expressive, mysterious eyes, and there is the sweet trace of a smile on his lips. There are faint signs of developing kidney tightness under the eyes, but not the dark shadows of the print. The earlobe is fuller, showing strong mental and physical vitality, while the gold ear ring represents not only a fashion statement but an unconscious stimulation of the kidneys and the pituitary gland. The collar and shirt are simple, almost Puritan, showing the portrait was composed in more informal conditions, probably in the theatre between rehearsals or performances.

The famous bust of Shakespeare in Stratford (*top left*) must also be considered in any discussion of the Bard's likenesses. It was executed by John Hall in 1748 and depicts a rather bloated man, with upward turning mustache and goatee, with his left hand on a manuscript and his right hand holding a quill. The bust—which Shakespearean scholar Dover Wilson compared to a "self-satisfied pork butcher"—represents an idealized image of Shakespeare in maturity or near the time of his death. The original bust on Shakespeare's tomb (*top right*) which it replaced was destroyed, but thanks to Dugdale's *Antiquities of Warwickshire,* published in 1656, we have a reproduction. It shows a more severe looking figure, with a triangular-shaped head, long mustache, and stern expression with his hands over a sack of some kind. Its portrayal of an entirely different person altogether—one who was more at home in the barn than on the stage and who fits the part of the squire who willed his wife his second best bed—only deepens the mystery.

## Shakespeare's Health

 s for Shakespeare's health and physical condition, we learn from the Sonnets that he was lame—perhaps from a fall on stage. In the preface to the First Folio, the printers eulogize his heavenly-sent genius and attest that they received his manuscripts with scarcely a blot. Curiously, the six surviving Shakespearean signatures contain three blots, not only mocking this claim, but occasioning several medical researchers to conclude that he had a stroke, palsy, or a chronic condition known as scrivener's hand.

In the absence of any surviving manuscripts, literary letters to or from the poet, or significant contemporary references to his wit and creative skill, we are left primarily with a few legal forms and miscellaneous commercial scraps to document his existence. Interestingly, several of these mention agricultural products. The main income of Stratford, a sleepy agricultural town, came from barley, and both John Shakespeare, his father, and Shakespeare in his later years invested and speculated in grain and other crops. In 1598, Shakespeare was accused of hoarding 70 bushels of corn and malt by the Privy Council and named among "the wicked people, in conditions more like to wolves, than natural men." This verdict, leveled in an era of plague and famine, is a severe blot on Shakespeare's character and one at odds with the generous, "fair, kind, and true" poet we have come to expect. It is, however, vaguely suggestive of the miserly looking country burgher staring out from the original bust in the Holy Trinity Church in Stratford. Perhaps the sack he is clutching is an ironic commentary on this or similar incidents.

Born on April 23, 1564, Shakespeare was a Four Tree. Like Columbus, he was very idealistic, romantic, and impressionable, easily given to letting his heart overrule his reason. In the Oriental zodiac, Shakespeare was a rat. Rat people are bright, inventive, and resourceful. According to legend, the Buddha held a race to rank the animals, and the lumbering ox, the strongest and most persevering of the contestants, was about to cross the finish line when the clever rat, who had hitchhiked on his back, jumped off to win the race, thus ranking him first in the Far Eastern zodiac and the ox second. In any event, rat types are very imaginative, intelligent, and usually find a way to prevail. However, they also tend to be furtive and secretive, and their quickness to act and tendency to collect and store up things for the future is often viewed by others as selfishness.

As *Hamlet* and the other plays show, Shakespeare was deeply rooted in the traditional way of eating. From his portraits, as well as literary works, we may conclude that he ate simply, mostly grain and vegetable quality food. His main staples were barley, wheat, oats, and rye, including dark sourdough bread (the food mentioned more frequently in the plays than any other). These grains, along with beans, vegetables, and occasional animal food, were cooked primarily in stews, creating a well rounded, well nourished personality and character. By nature active and energetic, the author of the plays was moderately attracted to yin to relax, especially salad, fruit (notably 'apricocks'), and wines (though more sour than sweet). Overall, he ate little meat, poultry, and other animal food and not much sugar, spices, or other strong condiments.

# Christopher Marlowe, Soulmate

 n 1953, an Elizabethan portrait was found in Corpus Christi College by workmen renovating an old Cambridge University dormitory. The painting, dated 1585, is believed to be that of Christopher Marlowe, the poet and playwright whose "mighty line" prefigured Shakespeare's and whom history records as dying tragically in 1593 in a tavern brawl. Born in 1564, several months earlier than Shakespeare—and thus also a Four Tree Rat—Marlowe studied at Corpus Christi at the time the portrait was composed.

The painting shows a poised, self-confident young man radiating an aura of invincibility. The almond-shaped eyes are observant, passionate, and fearless. The hair—long, thick, and fashionably swept back—conveys a sense of overall power and majesty, while the strand curving down on the left and the unruly curl on the collar add a devil-may-care hint of the rebelliousness within. The embroidered gold doublet is far too expensive for an undergraduate, especially a poor cobbler's son on scholarship. But then Kit Marlowe was no ordinary student. During his Cambridge years, he provided Queen Elizabeth's secret service with intelligence on religious and political intrigues while hobnobbing with the literati, and had sovereigns to spend.

The similarities between Marlowe's portrait and Shakespeare's are striking. Although the Stratford actor depicted in the Droeshout engraving is about twenty years older than the Cambridge classicist, we see the same basic features: the oval shape of the head, the wavy hairstyle, the thick gentle brows, the thin moustache, the faint beard, the symmetrical lips with slight puffiness on the right side, the long, well proportioned nose, and the searching eyes. Even the dominant grandparents—represented by the contracted inner right eye and outer left eye—are the same. (Marlowe also reputedly had a limp.)

Could Shakespeare's portrait be that of Marlowe? Could Marlowe be the real author of the Shakespearean canon? From a literary view, many scholars believe that Marlowe—the dazzling author of *Tamburlaine, Dr. Faustus, The Jew of Malta,* and other plays and the most popular playwright of the era—could have written the Shakespeare plays had he only lived. Marlowe and Shakespeare's leading sources, Ovid and Holinshed, are the same. The two poets' styles, subject matter, ambivalent sexuality, and passionate intensity are similar. Barabas, Tamburlaine, Dr. Faustus, Dido, Edward II, and Marlowe's other main characters reappear in new guise as Shylock, Othello/Iago, Prospero, Cleopatra, and Henry VI.

In the early 1590s, Marlowe reigned on the London stage as "the Muse's darling," while Shakespeare remained an unknown actor. Then a scant four months after Marlowe's death in a brawl at age twenty-nine, the first poem in Shakespeare's name appears, followed by one brilliant play after the other. The Stratford actor picks up where Marlowe leaves off. The chronology, the literary continuity, the dramatic fit are exact. Except for his premature death, attested to by the Queen's Coroner and sixteen solid citizens who formed the inquest, Marlowe would be the prime candidate for the laurels.

# Diet and Health:
# Shakespeare's Cook

*"Unquiet meals make ill digestions."*
—The Comedy of Errors

Will Shakespeare lived apart from his family for most of his acting career, and we don't know where he ate or who cooked his food. However, there is a clue. In the early 1600s, he was living in Silver Street in London with the Mountjoies, a Huguenot family, and was called to testify in a lawsuit brought by another lodger, Stephen Belott, who had married the couple's daughter. Belott sued his father-in-law, Christopher Mountjoie, a tiremaker, complaining his wife's dowry was less than expected.

Shakespeare refused to take sides, testifying that he had known both parties in the suit for ten years and both had behaved with goodwill and affection for each other. The salient point is that the lawsuit was brought following the death of Marie Mountjoie, the wife and mother-in-law of the principals. This suggests that over the previous decade her simple, well-balanced cooking kept peace in the household, but that upon her death all hell broke loose. Presumably, Shakespeare ate breakfast or the evening meal with the family during this time.

As Protestant refugees from France, the family would probably still have enjoyed simple French cooking, including the pancakes, salets (salads), and savory sauces that appear in Shakespeare's works. The poet's implied scorn of heavy English cooking—*Love's Labor Lost's* "greasy Joan doth keel the pot" and *As You Like It's* "fat and greasy citizens"—could stem from this contrast. In any event, Marie Mountjoie may be the real invisible hand behind *Hamlet* and the other masterpieces. ❖

# "What Nourishes Me, Destroys Me"

 clue to the mystery of Shakespeare's identity is the inscription on the Marlovian portrait. At the top left corner, beneath the date, is a Latin motto: *Quod me nutrit me destruit,* or "What nourishes me, destroys me." Literary critics interpret this as referring to passion, unrequited love, the Muse of poetry, or other transcendent ideal. The aphorism is original with Marlowe; it is not found in classical literature. However, it is found in Shakespeare's Sonnet #73: "Consumed with that which it was nourished by." The context is one of the aging poet contemplating the ephemerality of life and seeing the fire of youth and love expire and turn into ashes. A variant of the proverb is also found in Shakespeare's Pericles: *Quod me alit me extinguit.* ("That which lights me extinguishes me.") The odds of two poets coming up with the same aphorism—though less than that of the proverbial monkey pounding out *Hamlet* on the typewriter—are still astronomical.

At the most basic level, the motto centers on food and nourishment. It confirms everything that we have seen in *Hamlet,* the other plays, and in the visages of Shakespeare and Marlowe concerning the central importance of a well balanced diet and moderate way of life. Despite his strong, grain-based constitution, it can be objected that Marlowe was anything but moderate. His plays celebrated irony and the exotic, flirted with impiety and atheism, and bordered on dissent and sedition. Yet they did so in such a sweet, provocative, powerful way that they escaped the censor's pen and won widespread popular acclaim.

What accounts for Marlowe's defiant spirit? In the buttery records of Cambridge, young Marlowe's food expenses are preserved. One entry in 1580, for example, notes that he spent money on porridge of oatmeal and beef broth, one pence on beef, and a couple rations of beer. This mix of simple traditional and expensive aristocratic fare is just what we would expect from a young iconoclast. Though his staple food remained primarily whole grains and vegetable stews, he enjoyed beef and other fashionable foods when he could afford it and very likely drank like a fish. The cockiness of the portrait, the arrogance of the early plays, Marlowe's penchant for quarrels and violent disputes—all can be attributed to indulging in meat and alcohol in his youth and early adulthood.

## Marlowe's Arrest and 'Murder'

n May 18, 1593, Marlowe was suddenly arrested by the Star Chamber under suspicion of heresy and ordered to report daily to the Privy Council. The victims of this dread inquisitorial court included his fellow poet and friend Thomas Kyd, who implicated Marlowe under torture, and Francis Kett, a fellow Cambridge graduate, who was burned at the stake for heresy. On May 30, just twelve days after his arrest, Marlowe was killed in an altercation in Deptford, the town upriver from London. Had he not been fatally knifed in the eye and died instantly, he would very likely have had his "conscience scraped"—tortured—and been burned at the stake as a heretic. From the orthodox theological view, Marlowe's timely death manifested both God's justice and mercy—an irony not lost on his detractors.

The Archbishop of Canterbury, the powerful head of the Church of England, presided over the Star Chamber. John Whitgift, the Archbishop of Canturbury (*see inset*), was a stern disciplinarian. In one of his defenses of the faith, he solemnly warned, "I do charge all men before God and his angels, as they will answer at the day of judgment, that under the pretext of zeal they seek not to spoil the church . . . [and] nourish not contempt of magistrates, popularity, anabaptistry, and sundry other pernicious and pestilent errors." In 1586, he promulgated a rigorous edict, known as the Star Chamber Decree, which forbade all public criticism of the Church. Whitgift bore the hallmarks of a grand inquisitor. His arched eyebrows show a belligerent temperament, liver lines between the eyebrows indicate anger and hatred, the swollen nose corresponds with advanced heart disease and rigid, fixed opinions, and the darkness under the eyes shows tight kidneys and developing paranoia. Clearly, as Marlowe, a perceptive student of physiognomy, described an earlier, villainous Archbishop of Canturbury in *Edward II*, "His countenance bewrays he is displeased." His Grace, Lord Whitgift was a not a man to pardon the youthful folly of a strutting player (from Canturbury!) who denied the Trinity and mocked God's wounds. "In his examination of prisoners," the English *Dictionary of National Biography* informs us, "he showed a brutal insolence which is alien to all modern conceptions of justice or religion." And what did Whitgift and the other inquisitors nourish themselves on? "After each sitting, the Lords dined together in the Inner Star Chamber at the public expense," another account relates. "There are records of sumptuous banquets with rare and expensive delicacies and extravagant quantities of flesh and fish."

In the rapid turn of events between his arrest and death, partisans of Marlowe as Shakespeare see a plot afoot in which his murder was faked, Marlowe fled to the Continent, and fresh plays were subsequently sent back to England to appear under the name of a journeyman actor by the name of Will Shakespeare. Who better to stage-manage a murderous brawl than the nation's leading dramatist? What better way to survive than write the plays—Cyrano de Bergerac-like—under the disguise of a prosaic country actor who had come up to the capital to seek his fortune on the London stage?

The prologue to Marlowe's most popular play, *The Jew of Malta*, believed to have been added to the original text when it first appeared in print in 1598, hints at this scenario:

> *Albeit the world thinks Machiavel is dead,*
> *Yet was his soul but flown beyond the Alps,*
> *And now the Guise is dead, is come from France,*
> *To view this land, and frolic with his friends.*
> *To some perhaps my name is odious,*
> *But such as love me guard me from their tongues;*
> *And let them know that I am Machiavel,*
> *And weigh not men, and therefore not men's words.*
> *Admired I am of those that hate me most,*
> *Though some speak openly against my books,*
> *And they will read me, and thereby attain*
> *To Peter's chair: and when they cast me off,*
> *Are poisoned by my climbing followers.*
> *I count religion but a childish toy,*
> *And hold there is no sin but ignorance.*
> *Birds of the air will tell of murders past!*
> *I am ashamed to hear such fooleries . . .*
> *But whither am I bound? I come not, I,*
> *To read a lecture here in Britain,*
> *But to present the tragedy of a Jew . . .*

Machiavel refers to Machiavelli, the author of *The Prince*, and was one of the popular nicknames by which Marlowe was known. The Guise refers to the chief inquisitor of France, but generically to all persecutors and torturers such as the Star Chamber's. According to this interpretation, Marlowe fled beyond the Alps to Italy, where he lived and wrote in exile for several years, before returning—like the Wandering Jew he had become—incognito to England. Shakespeare's early comedies such as *The Taming of the Shrew, The Two Gentlemen of Verona, Romeo and Juliet,* and *The Merchant of Venice* take place in Italy, and scholars have long been puzzled at how he could have accumulated such a wealth of geographical detail about the Italian peninsula.

From a dietary view, an Italian sojourn would help explain the maturation of the early Shakespeare. In Italy, alone and unknown except for a few trusted contacts, Marlowe probably would have eaten in a lighter vein, acquiring a taste for pasta primavera, minestrone, and other lighter fare. Aside from the sobering close brush with death in England, a mellower diet, especially one that featured less animal food, would have purged much of the impetuosity, violence, and recklessness that characterized Marlowe's early writing and personal life. The milder climate, along with a change in diet, may also have moderated his sexual appetite.

In *As You Like It*, Shakespeare quotes Marlowe's most famous lines: "Dead shepherd now I find thy saw of might,/'Who ever loved that loved not at first sight?'" He also alludes, as scholars agree, to Marlowe's death with the phrase, "it strikes a man more dead than a great reckoning in a little room." The word "reckoning" was used in the official Coroner's report on the circumstances surrounding Marlowe's death. It refers to the fatal argument over paying the bill, or tally, for supper at which Marlowe was stabbed to death. According to Ingram Frizer's sworn testimony, he was sitting at table with his back turned to Marlowe, when the poet seized Frizer's knife and struck him from behind. Warding off the blow, Frizer gained possession of the weapon and struck Marlowe above the right eye, from which he died instantly. Robert Poley and Nicholas Skeres, the two other men present, corroborated the account. Interestingly, the Coroner's report was not discovered and published until 1925 and the earliest contemporary account of Marlowe's death notes he died of the plague. Thus the author of *As You Like It*, perhaps through a patron or high government contact, had access to the official record, suggesting further collusion of some kind. Altogether there are over 200 direct quotations, parallels, and echoes of Mar-

## Nine Star Ki:
# The Reckoning

Marlowe's arrest for heresy and "death" took place in 1593, a Two Soil year, which was gentle and peaceful overall. During May, Eight Soil—the unexpected—was in the center of the Ki flow, and Marlowe, a Four Tree, was in the One Water house, the house of darkness and difficulties. The best way to survive such a time is to turn within and avoid conflict, especially with authority, repre-

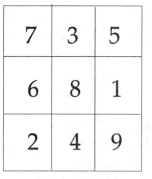

| 7 | 3 | 5 |
|---|---|---|
| 6 | 8 | 1 |
| 2 | 4 | 9 |

**May, 1593**

sented by Five Soil. In the Seven-Metal harvest spot for the year as a whole, Marlowe could have reaped an early death or —by virtue of strong intuition—escaped to write anew. ❖

owe's writings in Shakespeare's works, and the themes of betrayal, exile, and disguise course through the plots and characterizations of the thirty-seven plays like a single thread. As John Bakeless pointed out in *The Tragicall History of Christopher Marlowe*, his magisterial two-volume biography of Marlowe, Shakespeare drew on Marlowe's play *Dido* for the Player King's speech in *Hamlet* and the unique manner in which Claudius murdered King Hamlet is taken from a similar act of villainy in Marlowe's *Edward II*:

> . . . *To take a quill*
> *And blowe a little powder in his eares* . . .

Calvin Hoffman's book, *The Murder of the Man Who Was Shakespeare*, written in the mid-1950s, presents the most complete case for Marlowe's authorship of the Shakespearean canon. However, he makes many assumptions—such as another man, probably a sailor from Deptford, was murdered in Marlowe's stead and Marlowe had a homosexual relationship with his patron—which are unnecessary and unconvincing. In his play, *The Laurel Bough*, Sherwood Silliman suggests a look-a-like actor was killed in Marlowe's place, and he

# *Myth and Reality:*
# The Elizabethan Era

 Elizabethan England featured three principal theatres: 1) the Court itself, whose royal glory, dramatic intrigues, and ceremonial pomp riveted the nation; 2) the public mutilations, burnings, and hangings for witchcraft and heresy; and 3) the London stage.

As absolute sovereign, Elizabeth I presided over all three spectacles, directly governing Britain's foreign and domestic policy, sanctioning punishments and executions, and through her censor lifting or closing the curtain on the Globe and other playhouses.

Born on September 7, 1533, an Eight Soil, Elizabeth was constitutionally well suited to this task. The daughter of Henry VIII and the ill-starred Anne Boleyn, Elizabeth grew up in the shadow of her older half-sister, Mary Tudor. Inheriting a combination of yin and yang qualities from her parents, the little girl had reddish golden hair, long hands, and grew up upright, dignified, and controlled. Elizabeth's early governess protected her from "divers meats, and fruits, and wine" at a young age, so that she developed the self-discipline foreign to her immensely fat, corpulent father. She mastered several languages, played the virginal, and sang and danced. However, her later governess was not so strict, and as a young lady she suffered from violent headaches (more yin) and missed menstrual periods (more yang).

For two years, Elizabeth languished in the Tower of London, under threat of execution as a rival to the throne. But with the death of Mary, a staunch Catholic, from ovarian cancer, she was crowned in 1558 and acclaimed as the queen who would restore Protestant worship. Over the next fifty years, Elizabeth navigated the ship of state through the shoals of religious conflict, foiling plots by Catholics to seize the throne, avoiding foreign wars with Spain and France, and tempering Puritan zealotry.

To maintain power, Elizabeth's way of eating became increasingly extreme. Though she ate little meat, she consumed plenty of chicken, game birds, and fish. On one five-day royal visit to a country estate, the Queen's entourage consumed the following provisions: 60 sheep, 34 lambs, 26 pigs, 18 calves, 8 oxen, 10 kids and dozens of birds: over 350 chickens, more than 200 pigeons, 12 dozen ducklings and herons, 10 dozen geese, 16 dozen quails, as well as quantities of capons, pullets, bitterns, partridges, larks, curlews, shoveles, pheasants, and mallards.

Over the years, the Queen grew harder and more rigid as a result of this heavy yang, animal food diet. She issued an injunction to stamp out "diversity, variety and vain love of singularity from the Church." Beginning in 1573, several Puritan phamphleteers were burned at the stake and printers who published unlicensed material had their hands chopped off. Catholics, suspected heretics, and other nonconformists were put to the rack and tortured, and, after a long period of captivity, Mary Queen of Scots was finally beheaded. To this day, historians are divided whether she was part of a genuine plot to overthrow Elizabeth or whether she was framed by Sir Francis Walsingham, the head of Elizabeth's secret service, and William Cecil, the Lord Treasurer, whose Machiavellian cunning was perfectly nuanced to their monarch's bidding. Yet even they felt Elizabeth's capriciousness, as she hen-pecked her senior ministers, slapped her ladies in waiting, and imprisoned her suitors for making love to other women. To relax, she enjoyed riding and hunting deer which she slew herself. As her symbol, she adopted the falcon, the bird of prey of which the female of the species is larger than the male.

To offset her yang diet, Elizabeth enjoyed fine white bread, sweetmeats; sugary cakes, custards, and puddings; and other soft, delicious yin fare. The combination of extremes gradually took its toll, and she became irresolute, hysterical, and subject to fainting fits. The last years of her reign were characterized by alternating tantrums against religious dissent and sexual license and charming interludes in which she sang, danced, and captivated her listeners with impromptu speeches in fluent Latin or Italian. In the end, however, paranoia won out, and one of the last sad images of Elizabeth is of her Hamlet-like plunging a sword into the hangings of her bedroom to foil imagined spies and assassins.

The era she presided over is famous for its flourishing of art and culture, the rise of England as a world power, and New World colonies. But these were as much a reaction, as a result, of her policies. Bred to power, wed to rule, and divorced from the traditional diet of humanity, Elizabeth governed with an iron hand, an unbending spirit, and largely untroubled conscience. ❖

had an affair with the wife of his patron. My grandfather's book, *Shakespeare, Thy Name Is Marlowe*, focuses on Marlowe's religious views and the charges of heresy brought against him and has a perceptive, commonsense discussion of the portraits and busts.

Through the early 1960s, historians and Shakespearean scholars dismissed the Marlovian theory as the fairy tale of a few malcontents and freethinkers like Hoffman, Silliman, and my grandfather, primarily on the grounds that it was unthinkable for the Queen's Coroner's report to have been doctored. (Hoffman's credibility plunged to absolute zero when he predicted the lost manuscripts of Shakespeare's plays would be found in the tomb of Marlowe's patron, Sir Thomas Walsingham. To the fanfare of the mass media and TV camera lights, the sarcophagus was opened—and found to be empty!) However, following the Kennedy assassination, Watergate, the surfacing of Cold War secrets, and fresh information on the three men who were with Marlowe at the time of his death, a conspiracy to stage his death and conceal the authorship today seems more likely. All three of Marlowe's dinner companions were government spies, informers, or double agents. They were all associates or in the employ of Thomas Walsingham, the brother of Sir Francis Walsingham, the longtime head of Elizabeth's secret service, and they remained so after the murder! Not only is this highly suspect, but Ingrim Frizer, Marlowe's assailant, received an official pardon for acting in self-defense and was freed from prison in record time. In an era before telephones and rapid transportation, the inquest and burial itself were convened, conducted, and concluded in an improbable 18 hours of the time of death. Mrs. Bull, at whose lodgings and private inn the stabbing took place, was related to the Cecils, the Queen's senior ministers who could have masterminded the entire affair. Modern surgeons who have examined the Coroner's report say that it is impossible for such a wound to kill instantaneously. The inconsistencies, coincidences, improbabilities, and contradictions go on and on.

Interestingly, in *Hamlet*, the clowns in the famous gravediggers' scene mock the Coroner's law in a dialogue on the legal meaning of suicide:

SECOND CLOWN: *But is this law?*
FIRST CLOWN: *Ay, marry, it's; crowner's quest law.*

# Insights from the I Ching

onspiracy or coincidence? Did Marlowe live or die? I consulted the *I Ching* about his fate and received hexagram 64 Before Completion changing to hexagram 50 The Cauldron. The moving line in the third place reads:

*Before completion, attack brings misfortune.*
*It furthers one to cross the great water.*

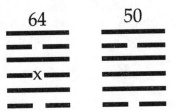

The commentary goes on to explain, "A new situation must be created; one must engage the energies of able helpers and in fellowship take this decisive step—cross the great water. Then completion is possible." Confucius' commentary adds, "One should not attempt to force completion but should try to get clear of the whole situation. A change of character is necessary." The entire situation changed into the Cauldron, the hexagram representing the highest literature and art.

What of the role of Will Shakespeare, the actor? In line two of hexagram 37 The Family, the *I Ching* likens him to an able helpmate, a "wife who must always be guided by the will of the master of the house." By attending to the duties at hand, the subordinate "becomes the center of social and religious life of the family, and [his] perseverance in this position brings good fortune to the whole house."

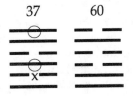

Marlowe's own legacy is described in the top line of this hexagram: "His work commands respect. In the end good fortune comes." Commenting on the dynamic between the two men, the *I Ching* further observed in hexagram 25 Innocence, the Unexpected: "Undeserved misfortune. The cow tethered by someone is the wanderer's gain, the citizen's loss." The plays written by Marlowe were taken up by Shakespeare and he reaped the honors.

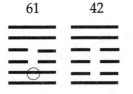

Are these events alluded to in Shakespeare's plays and poems? The *I Ching* replied with hexagram 61 Inner Truth, line 2: "A crane calling in the shade. Its young answers it. I have a good goblet. I will share it with you." The commentary states: "This refers to the involuntary influence of a man's inner being upon persons of kindred spirit. The crane need not show itself on a high hill. It may be quite hidden when it sounds its call; yet its young will hear its note, will recognize it and give answer." In the mighty lines, the marvelous characterizations, the musical, fugue-like plots, the sweet melodies of the true author are easily recognizable.

Finally, if the Shakespeare engraving really depicts Marlowe, why was it put in the First Folio? In the thirty years that passed between Marlowe's "death" and the publication of Shakespeare's collected works, had the inquisitors—as well as the Queen—died? Had the danger passed?

To this inquiry, I received hexagram 53 Gradual Progress with moving lines in the third, fourth, and fifth places indicating that 1) a young man plunged rashly into a struggle and jeopardized his own life, 2) after warding off an unjustified attack a safe place was found in which life could continue de-

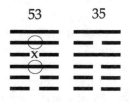

spite the danger, and 3) despite isolation and misunderstandings, reconciliation was achieved and a union (of portrait and verse?) based on natural affinity prevailed.

Sometimes *The Book of Change's* readings are enigmatic and open to multiple interpretations. But in this case, approaching the subject from different angles, the replies all consistently point to Marlowe being the author of the works attributed to Shakespeare. The outcomes—hexagrams 50, 60, 13, 42, and 35—are all highly fortunate.

# The Mysterious Mr. W.H.

n his new book *The Reckoning: The Murder of Christopher Marlowe*, Charles Nichols, on the basis of fresh evidence, sketches the broad outlines of the events leading up to Marlowe's arrest. He concludes that Marlowe was a pawn in the larger struggle between two powerful lords, the Earl of Essex and Sir Walter Raleigh who were competing for the favor of Queen Elizabeth, and their circles at Court. Nichols believes that Marlowe, an associate of Raleigh, was framed by the Essex faction to discredit the famed explorer and soldier of fortune. As a sometime spy, Marlowe's atheism was largely feigned, but Essex's side tarred him with the brush of heresy to skewer Raleigh, whose views on religious liberty already bordered on the nonconformist. Marlowe was served up to the witchhunters of the Star Chamber. Even then, Raleigh, the Cecils, or other highly placed protectors could probably have smoothed things over (they did get Marlowe released on personal bond), but the charges were brought to the personal attention of the Queen. From that point on, even Lord Burghley, the senior minister, would have been powerless to get in between what is referred to in *King Lear* as "the dragon and [her] wrath."

Nichols accepts the conventional view that Marlowe met his end in Deptford, though he shows that there were so many double and triple agents and levels of deception involved that anything could have happened. The person who evidently saved Marlowe's life was his patron, Thomas Walsingham, at whose home in Scadbury House in Chislehurst, 12 miles southeast of London, Marlowe at the time was living and writing. Commenting on Walsingham's role, the *I Ching* observed in hexagram 58, line 5: "Dangerous elements approach even the best of men. If a man permits himself to have anything to do with them, their disintegrating influence acts slowly but surely, and inevitably brings dangers in its train. But if he recognizes the situation and can comprehend the danger, he knows how to protect himself [and his friends] and remain unharmed."

How was this accomplished? In hexagram 12 Standstill, line 4, the *I Ching* reveals: "He who acts at the command of the highest remains without blame. Those of like mind partake of the blessing."

The commentary goes on to explain that this means "the minister and ruler were united." The ruler would be Walsingham and the ministers of like mind the three agents, Frizer, Skeres, and Poley, who staged Marlowe's "death."

A passage in Marlowe's *Edward II* about a conspiracy may have suggested the deception, especially the attack with a knife:

> But were he [Gaveston, the poetic friend of the king]
>   here, detested as he is,
> How easily might some base slave be suborned
> To greet his lordship with a poniard,
> And none so much as blame the murdered,
> But rather praise him for that brave attempt,
> And in the chronicle enrol his name
> For purging of the realm of such a plague!

We find another parallel to this scenario in *Measure for Measure* when Angelo, the inflexible deputy ruler, orders the head of Claudio, the hapless lover, brought to him. Friar Lodowick (the real Duke in disguise) persuades the Provost of the prison to hide Claudio and substitutes the head of another prisoner who has died a natural death. "O death's a great disguiser," the Friar exclaims.

Walsingham, who appears to have orchestrated the fake death, engineered Marlowe's escape to Europe, and furnished him with living expenses, would also appear to be the mysterious Mr. W. H. to whom the Shakespearean Sonnets are dedicated. (Washingham's name was often spelled Walsing-Ham, just as Shakespeare was most commonly spelled Shake-Speare.) The Sonnets—soliloquies of the poet's innermost thoughts—are filled with references to these events and voice the deep emotions of loss, bitterness, regret, love and gratitude (to his patron), and hope (of returning to England) that the poet experienced. For example, Sonnet 29 begins:

> When, in disgrace with fortune and men's eyes,
> I all alone beweep my outcast state,
> And trouble deaf heaven with my bootless cries,
> And look upon myself and curse my fate . . .

# Scientific Method:
# Shakespeare's Literary Fingerprint

Dr. Thomas Mendenhall, a professor of physics at Ohio State University and president of the American Association for the Advancement of Science, discovered that everyone has a unique "literary fingerprint." By counting the number of letters in the words of an author's corpus—whether prose or poetry, a letter or an novel—and plotting

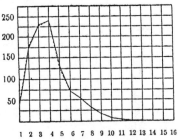

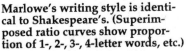

**Marlowe's writing style is identical to Shakespeare's. (Superimposed ratio curves show proportion of 1-, 2-, 3-, 4-letter words, etc.)**

them on a graph, a unique individual ratio-curve appears. No two people have exactly the same graph; thus given a sufficient minimum number of words (e.g., 100,000), the real identity of a disputed or anonymous writing can be ascertained.

Hired early in the century by a prominent Baconian to compare the Shakespearean canon with the works of Francis Bacon, a leading contender for the crown, Mendenhall hired a team of young women to manually count several million words in the First Folio, Bacon's output, and as a control the writings of other Elizabethan poets. To the disappointment of his patron, but not surprisingly to anyone who has read Bacon's turgid prose, he found that Bacon's ratio-curve was miles apart from Shakespeare's. However, the tedious undertaking—all the more momentous for having been completed in the pre-computer era—did not go for nought. "It was in the counting and plotting of the plays of Christopher Marlowe, however, that something akin to a sensation was produced among those actually engaged in the work," Mendenhall reported in an article "A Mechanical Solution for a Literary Problem," in the *Popular Science Monthly* in December, 1901. ". . . In the characteristic curves of his plays Christopher Marlowe agrees with Shakespeare as well as Shakespeare agrees with himself." ❖

There is nothing in the life of William Shakespeare the actor that we know of—or can imagine—to evoke such a *cri du coeur*.

In Sonnet 76, the poet confesses:

> *That every word doth almost tell my name,*
> *Showing their birth and where they did proceed?*

Most scholars identify the mysterious rival poet in Sonnets 81-83 as Marlowe himself. But some of the references are clearly to Shakespeare the actor!

> *When you entombed in men's eyes shall be.*
> *Your monument shall be my gentle verse . . .*
> *You still shall live—such virtue hath my pen— . . .*

The word "entombed" which we associate with the crypt and bust in Stratford is a prophetic touch.

## The Dark Lady of the Sonnets

nother series of twenty-six poems revolves around a woman popularly known as the Dark Lady of the Sonnets. She was not only dark complexioned—"my mistress' eyes are raven black/Her brows so suited, and they mourners seem"—but also cruel and merciless. This combination proved irresistible, and Marlowe/Shakespeare* immortalizes his obsession with her in some of the most beautiful love poetry in the English language. We learn few details about the mysterious lady, except that she is high-born, married, and plays the virginal (a lute-like instrument).

Who was she? Scholars have advanced a dozen candidates, but none is especially convincing. When we think of her power over her lover, we immediately think of the poet's epigram: "What nourishes me, destroys me," and famous lines from the plays such as *Twelfth Night's*, "If music be the food of love, play on." In Marlowe/

---

*\*Marlowe/Shakespeare refers to Marlowe's presumed life from May 30, 1593 on, during which he wrote the plays under Shakespeare's name.*

Shakespeare's life and writings, the images of food and love are intertwined. Clearly, whoever the Dark Lady was she did not cook for herself—or her suitor. In this respect she was a modern woman, the poet's dark half, Shakespeare's Mona Lisa.

Turning to the *I Ching* for insight on their relationship, we are directed to hexagram 6 Conflict, lines 2 and 3. The commentary on the first moving line reads: "In a struggle with an enemy of superior strength, retreat is no disgrace. Timely withdrawal prevents bad consequences. If, out of a false sense of honor, a man allowed himself to be tempted into an unequal conflict, he would be drawing down disaster upon himself. In such a case a wise and conciliatory attitude benefits the whole community, which will then not be drawn into the conflict." The "unequal conflict" alludes to a vast difference in social standing between the poet and his love. Heeding, for once, his mind rather than his heart, Marlowe/Shakespeare wisely withdrew, forestalling not only further heartache but the wrath of his paramour's husband, the Queen, and the Court.

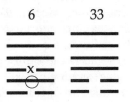

Line 3 relates that the poet went on to "nourish [him]self on ancient virtue." Sublimating his love, the poet transmuted it into immortal verse. *The Book of Change* goes on to laud the poet's selfless choice: "Whatever a man possess through the strength of his own nature cannot be lost. If one enters the service of a superior, one can avoid conflict only by not seeking works for the sake of prestige. It is enough if the work is done: let the honor go to the other." Like Bassanio in *The Merchant of Venice,* the poet chose the simple leaden casket in which love, beauty, and art are their own rewards, spurning the gold and silver trappings of power, fame, and wealth.

One possible candidate for the dark mistress is Lady Mary Sidney, the Countess of Pembroke. She was the sister of the poet and fallen war hero Sir Philip Sidney; the wife of Henry Herbert, the Earl of Pembroke; and an accomplished poet and playwright in her own right (one of her translations may be a source for *Antony and Cleopatra*). As a Seven Metal (born in 1561, just three years earlier than the poet), her energy naturally suppressed that of Marlowe who was a Four Tree. In 1592, the year prior to his arrest, Marlowe wrote a letter to the Countess in a tribute to his late friend and fellow poet Thomas Watson in which he addressed her as "the Most Illustrious Noble Lady, adorned with all gifts both of mind and body." In the supplicatory fashion of the time, he referred to her as the "true sister of Sidney the bard of Apollo, fostering parent of letters, . . . Muse of the Poets of our time . . . . " Calling upon her to bless the memory of his friend, Marlowe continues: "And though thy glorious name is spread abroad not only among us but even among foreign nations, too far ever to be destroyed by the rusty antiquity of Time, or added to by the praise of mortals (for how can anything be

**Mary Sidney,
the Countess of Pembroke**

greater than what is infinite?), yet, crowned as thou art by the songs of many as by a starry diadem Ariadne, scorn not this pure priest of Phoebus bestowing another star upon thy crown . . . "

The image of Time, with his rusty scythe, as the destroyer and devourer of life, finds dozens of echoes in the Shakespearean Sonnets, but the most remarkable parallel is between the sentiments expressed here and those in *As You Like It*. In this Shakespearean play about an exiled king and his court who have been banished into the forest by a usurping ruler, there appears a young woman by the name of Phoebe. She is the object of the affection of Silvius, a young flockherder whose fair looks, occupation (shepherd = poet), and lovesick demeanor remind us of Marlowe, who is eulogized, as we noted earlier, as "the dead shepherd" in the very same play. In Greek mythology, Phoebe is the twin sister of Apollo and plays the moon to his sun. In the letter to the Countess, as we have just noted, Marlowe calls her "true sister of Sidney the bard of Apollo," thus equating her with Phoebe!

In the play, Phoebe does not much care for Silvius and dismisses one of his letters (read sonnets):

> He said mine eyes were black and my hair black
> And, now I am remembered, scorned at me.
> I marvel why I answered not again.

The word "scorn" echoes the line in the letter "scorn not this pure priest of Phoebus [Apollo]." Only when Rosalind tricks Phoebe into pledging her troth does she begrudgingly accept Silvius as her mate. As the editor of her brother's celebrated epic, *Arcadia*, we find the

# Fortune's Wheel

The Elizabethan Age fell within the 81-year Nine Star Ki cycle—1550-1631—governed by Five Soil energy. During such an era, power, war and peace, and basic health and existence are at center stage. Perfectly mirroring this social and environmental energy, the Shakespearean plays end in either complete destruction or unification. In *Hamlet, Othello, Macbeth, King Lear,* and other tragedies, everyone dies. In *The Merchant of Venice, As You Like It, Much Ado About Nothing, Measure for Measure,* and other comedies, everyone marries.     ❖

Arden Forest in *As You Like It* the perfect pastoral setting for a *roman a clef* appearance of the the talented Countess of Pembroke. (In mythology, Silvius is the youngest son of Aeneas, the epic hero and founder of Rome, and this choice of name may be a clue to the poet's self-image as a pastoral swain and founder of a new Troy.)

Ever the passionate shepherd, Marlowe concluded the letter to the Countess beseeching her to watch over not only Watson but himself. "So shall I, whose slender wealth is but the seashore myrtle of Venus and Daphne's evergreen laurel, on the foremost page of every poem invoke thee as Mistress of the Muses to my aid: to sum up all, thy virtue, which shall overcome virtue herself, shall likewise overcome even eternity." Marlowe signed the dedicatory epistle, "Most desirous to do thee honour, C.M."

Whether Marlowe followed up his pledge to devote his future works to her we do not know, as the events at Deptford rapidly overtook him. The Countess of Pembroke, who played the lute, wrote sonnets, and had legions of admirers, was identified with poet Samuel Daniel, but patronized Nicholas Breton, Ben Jonson, and many others. Perhaps one of these appears in the rival poet sequences in the Sonnets. Or the rival poet could be her brother, Sir Philip Sidney, whose sonnets are considered superior to Shakespeare's, or finally Plutarch, the greatest sonnet writer of all, whose poems the Countess translated from the original Italian.

The Countess' brother, incidentally, was the son-in-law of Sir Frances Walsingham, the head of Elizabeth's secret service and brother of Thomas Walsingham, Marlowe's patron. Her uncle was Robert Dudley, the Earl of Leicester, the Queen's great love and most trusted adviser. Her husband, who had two previous wives, was twenty-five years older than she, and by the 1590s there were rumors at Court they were estranged. In 1603, Shakespeare's company visited Wilton, the Pembroke estate, and performed *As You Like It*. She wrote a letter noting "that fellow Shakspere"—a curious form of address if he were the illustrious playwright—was visiting.

As for having dark hair and looks, Lady Mary was a natural brunette, but liked to dress up in blond wigs. As one contemporary noted, she "Adorned her head with golden borrowed haire." The Shakespearean Sonnets mock the Dark Lady's use of cosmetics and vanity (the Elizabethan equivalent of blondes having more fun): "Fairing the foul with art's false borrowed face." Phoebe's indignant reaction to Silvius calling her eyes and hair black (when they are simply dark brown) echoes these sentiments. The poet also may have immortalized his love in "The Phoenix and the Turtle," one of Shakespeare's early love poems. After her brother's death, the Countess was known as "the Phoenix" because she completed his literary works and his spirit seemed to rise from the ashes. The turtle refers to the turtledove, a bird fabled for its constancy.

Thus all the threads of temporal and spiritual power, literature, spycraft, and love weave their magic through the poet's personal

## Elizabethan Nine Star Ki

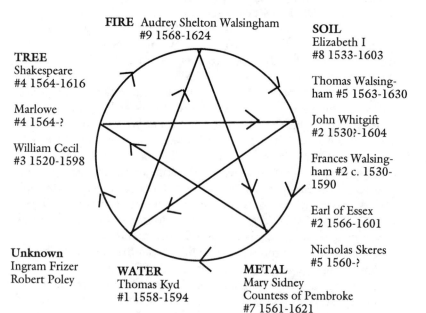

FIRE  Audrey Shelton Walsingham
#9 1568-1624

SOIL
Elizabeth I
#8 1533-1603

TREE
Shakespeare
#4 1564-1616

Marlowe
#4 1564-?

William Cecil
#3 1520-1598

Thomas Walsingham #5 1563-1630

John Whitgift
#2 1530?-1604

Frances Walsingham #2 c. 1530-1590

Earl of Essex
#2 1566-1601

Unknown
Ingram Frizer
Robert Poley

Nicholas Skeres
#5 1560-?

WATER
Thomas Kyd
#1 1558-1594

METAL
Mary Sidney
Countess of Pembroke
#7 1561-1621

Raleigh #7 1552-1618

drama. Whoever the Dark Lady was, like the seaweed begirting the waist of the Goddess of Love or the boughs adorning the celestial nymph, the poet's true love was the life-giving energy of nature herself, the sweet music of the spheres, the order of the infinite universe.

## The Golden Quill

 change in Marlowe/Shakespeare's exiled fortunes probably occurred in the late 1590s. In 1597, Queen Elizabeth visited Scadbury Park and knighted Thomas Walsingham. He had performed valuable military services that may have tempered any lingering feelings she bore for his part in the escape of Marlowe (if she had later knowledge of it). (Elizabeth's beleaguered ministers often ignored her direct commands or resorted to subterfuges until her pique subsided and the tempest passed.) The Queen's feelings for Walsingham in the early 1590s were probably ambivalent at best. His grandfather, Sir Edmund Walsingham, served as Lieutenant of the Tower in London and was the official who beheaded her mother, Anne Boleyn, when King Henry VIII discarded her for another wife. In the meanwhile, Walsingham married Audrey Shelton, whose grandparents had sheltered—and hence probably saved the life of—young Elizabeth when she was in peril from her half-sister Mary nearly a half century earlier. Elizabeth was eternally grateful to the Shelton family and after the marriage regularly feted Sir Thomas and Lady Audrey at Court.

In London, Kit Marlowe may have roomed (and boarded) with Will Shakespeare. It is amusing to imagine Marlowe/Shakespeare appearing before the Queen in one of the royal performances Shakespeare's troupe performed. I like to envision him playing Touchstone, the wise fool in *As You Like It*. A touchstone is a stone used to test for gold or silver—i.e., for truth. In the play, Touchstone is the character who delivers the lines about Marlowe's death—"a great reckoning in a little room"—and engages in dazzling word play with a country bumpkin by the name of William. He tells William (the only William among nearly one thousand characters in the Shakespearean plays):

# Marlowe's Lost Play

"All women are ambitious naturally," Marlowe observed in *Hero and Leander* in one of his most famous lines. The only copy of his play *The Maiden's Holiday,* an early comedy, was destroyed by an absent-minded cook. John Warburton, an eighteenth century collector of Elizabethan manuscripts, recorded that it was "unluckily burnd or put under pye bottoms" by his cook. Perhaps the good maiden—a modern woman—took a holiday from the kitchen herself, and the play met its just desserts. ❖

Then learn this of me: to have is to have. For it is a figure in rhetoric that drink, being poured out of a cup into a glass, by filling the one doth empty the other. For all your writers do consent that *ipse* [he himself] is he. Now, you are not *ipse* [he himself], for I am he.

He appears to be talking directly about authoring the plays and pouring them from his cup into another's. The sense is: Everyone thinks you, William, are the author; but you are not, for I am he.

Marlowe still had to be careful. In 1599, Archbishop Whitgift called in all satires and epigrammatic books and ordered them burned. At the top of his list was Marlowe's translation of Ovid. In any event, the political climate in England had changed. Essex, whose faction probably set Marlowe up for arrest, had fallen out of favor with the Queen. She took away his chief source of income, the monopoly on the import of sweet wines, and following his rash rebellion, he was confined to the Tower and executed. Elizabeth herself passed away in 1603 (with the Archbishop at her bedside), and King James of Scotland assumed the throne. Whitgift himself died the following year, stricken while dining at Whitehall, an ironic fate that probably was not lost on the author whose motto was "*Quod me nutrit me destruit.*"

Shakespeare's greatest plays were written in the Jacobean era, suggesting that in addition to the wisdom that comes with age, Marlowe/Shakespeare felt psychologically freer to circulate in London, though not use his real name. The mature plays show a greater sensitivity toward racial and religious prejudice, a more realistic understanding of the costs of power, and a concern for the continuity of the generations as opposed to flaunting parental authority, the theme of the youthful comedies. Shakespeare the actor died in 1616 in Stratford, where he had returned to live the life of a country squire, and no one in the world of arts and letters in London noted his passing. We don't know when Marlowe/Shakespeare died, but it was probably sometime shortly before 1623 when the First Folio came out. Edward Blount, the principal publisher, was a friend and admirer of Marlowe's and had brought out some of his earlier plays. (Thomas Thorpe, who published Shakespeare's Sonnets in 1609, had also previously published Marlowe.) It was probably Blount who had the audacity to include the engraving of Marlowe/Shakespeare on the frontispiece with the invitation to "looke not on his Picture [which was unknown to a generation of theatre-goers who would not recognize it] but upon his Booke." The First Folio, interestingly, was dedicated to William and Philip Herbert, the sons of Mary Herbert, the Countess of Pembroke.

From four standpoints—physiognomy, literary criticism, the *I Ching*, and modern statistical science—we have reviewed the authorship controversy and concluded that Shakespeare's "golden quill," as he calls it in the Sonnets, was really held by Christopher Marlowe. Blessed with a strong constitution and the intuition to return to a balanced, largely grain-and-vegetable-centered diet, the poet outwitted the ambitious courtiers—the Rosencrantzes and Guildensterns of Elizabeth's Court—and the pious, greasy, Claudius-like persecutors who would have sacrificed him on the altar of their own spiritual ignorance and worldly excess. Marlowe's relationship with the actor from Stratford, who produced the plays for the stage with his own flair and genius, is one of the great literary partnerships of all time.

The true story of Kit Marlowe's afterlife—the intrigues and betrayals, the flight and exile, the cover-up and literary disguise, the return and silent triumph—is more astonishing than *Hamlet* or any other play ever written in Shakespeare's name.

> *When to the sessions of sweet silent thought*
> *I summon up remembrance of things past,*
> *I sigh the lack of many a thing I sought,*
> *And with old woes new wail my dear time's waste . . .*
> > *But if the while I think of thee, dear friend,*
> > *All losses are restored and sorrows end.*
> > > —Sonnet 30 ❖

# The Author of *Hamlet*?

What did Marlowe/ Shakespeare look like when he wrote *Hamlet, Macbeth, Measure for Measure* and his other mature works? Thanks to modern computer graphics, we can glimpse the playwright as he looked like about 1595 to 1600 by combining the early portrait of Marlowe (see p. 103) and the later engraving of Shakespeare (see p. 81). A software program called Morph created a likeness of the poet as he may have appeared at the height of his genius. ❖

## Select Bibliography

Bakeless, John, *The Tragicall History of Christopher Marlowe*, Harvard University Press, 1942.

Greenblatt, Stephen, *Shakespearean Negotiations*, University of California Press, 1988.

Hannay, Margaret P., *Philip's Phoenix: Mary Sidney, Countess of Pembroke*, Oxford University Press, 1990.

Hibbert, Christopher, *The Virgin Queen: Elizabeth I, Genius of the Golden Age*, Addison Welsey, 1991.

Hoffman, Calvin, *The Murder of the Man Who Was Shakespeare*, Julian Messner, 1955.

Levi, Peter, *The Life and Times of William Shakespeare*, Henry Holt, 1988.

Nicholl, Charles, *The Reckoning: The Murder of Christopher Marlowe*, Harcourt Brace, 1992.

Rouse, A. L., *Christopher Marlowe*, Harper & Row, 1964.

Silliman, Sherwood E., *The Laurel Bough*, privately printed, 1956.

Williams, David Rhys, *Shakespeare, Thy Name Is Marlowe*, Philosophical Library, 1966.

Wright, A. D., and Virginia F. Stern, *In Search of Christopher Marlowe*, Vanguard, 1965.

# Afterword

Life exists within worlds of multiple spirals. From inconceivably large galaxies to invisibly minute subatomic particles, from solar systems to the helical strands of DNA, from the flow of wind and water to the formation and structure of plants and animals, all life is spirally constituted and governed. Not only individual human lives but also human history as a whole is subject to the laws of spiral motion and change. Antagonistic and complementary forces govern the development of human affairs, underlying wavelike patterns of growth and decay, health and sickness, peace and war.

The purpose of art, Hamlet observed, is to hold "the mirror up to nature." Leonardo's genius, Columbus' vision, and Marlowe/Shakespeare's wit reflected natural order, and in their achievements we intuitively recognize the universal laws of balance and harmony, the seamless union of complementary opposites, the timeless dance of yin and yang. Leonardo's canvases celebrate spirals, and throughout his life he studied this basic pattern in nature and the human form. Columbus, a keen observer in his own right, read spiral ocean currents, trade winds, and the flights of birds to reach his destination. Steeped in history and prophecy, myth and legend, the great navigator conceived his entire enterprise within the cyclical framework of rebuilding Zion and of a return to paradise. Marlowe/Shakespeare's plays—especially the comedies with their twin pairs of lovers, multiple reversals, shared recognitions, and final reunions—are logarithmic in structure. His thematic representation of girls disguised as boys (performed by boy actors dressed up as girls) mimics the subtle interplay of yin changing into yang, yang changing into yin. The restoration of order at the close of a performance—ending in marriage, a lifting of the plague, a bountiful harvest, and other blessings—is as much cosmic and social as romantic and personal in its healing vision.

Whole cereal grains, the foundation of human culture and civilization, shine through the life and thought of these Renaissance masters and help to explain their creativity and brilliance. However, he time in which they lived marked the beginning of the decline of the traditional way of eating and the rise of the modern diet. In childhood, youth, and early adulthood, whole grains, vegetables, and other fresh foods continued to be their principal food. But by middle age, the effects of consuming more animal food, polished grains, excessive fruit, sugar, spices, or other articles began to take a toll on their health and judgment. Impeding the smooth flow of heaven and earth's energy through the central channel, the organs, and the meridians, the modern diet clogs our bodies, clouds our minds, and gives rise to delusional thinking and behavior.

The steady, balanced flow of natural electromagnetic energy, or Ki, through the mind/body is a universal birthright. We see this especially in children, until about the age of ten, when they usually begin to lose their natural curiosity, boundless energy, and lack of self-consciousness. This is primarily a result of socialization and the modern way of life, including formal education.

Physical vitality goes hand in hand with aesthetic and spiritual comprehension. One cannot exist without the other. There is a marvelous aura of activity, playfulness, and spontaneity surrounding great artists and creative individuals. Leonardo's inventiveness, Columbus' prophetic faith, and Marlowe/Shakespeare's dazzling wit astonish us in an age which has sundered heaven and earth and neglected the basic order of nature.

Throughout history, artists, philosophers, prophets, shamans, and other highly creative persons have been able to sense or perceive images from the distant past or far future. Leonardo's seemingly effortless ability to go forward and backward in time flows from this source. Columbus' secret desire to fulfill Biblical prophecy harkens back to Eden and lost paradise. Like Ovid, his main source, Marlowe/Shakespeare's yearning for the return of the Golden Age runs through the plays and poems like a gentle melody.

Nearly two thousand years earlier, Hippocrates taught his students that in making a diagnosis, there are two basic questions to ask the patient: What do you eat, and who cooks your food? As we have seen, Leonardo, Columbus, and Marlowe/Shakespeare were semi-macrobiotic in their way of eating. But we do not know who cooked for them, and in that respect they are very modern indeed. It is possible that Leonardo kept a kitchen attached to his workshop and in between frescoes and inventions prepared his own millet or pasta. We can imagine Columbus occasionally boiling a pot of rice and beans on the dusty roads of Spain and on the forecastle of the caravel plying the Atlantic. And Marlowe/Shakespeare may have wielded a baking tin, soup ladle, and salad fork as deftly as he did a

# The Spiral of History

*Source: One Peaceful World by Michio Kushi and Alex Jack, St. Martin's Press, New York, 1987.*

pen. But it is doubtful they cooked for themselves regularly.

The women who nourished them remain largely anonymous. But next to their mothers, they are the real creators of our gifted spirits' life and work. They were humble, hard-working, and like the producer and director of a play, content to remain backstage, creators of the highest art. Fortunately the food they prepared was traditionally made and nourished the better angels of their nature. As the modern age progressed, the preparation of daily fare left home and family, and darker spirits prevailed. The arc of dietary excess extended from Florence, Barcelona, and London to Santo Domingo, Mexico City, and eventually Plymouth and New Amsterdam. With the rise of the Industrial Revolution, humanity's greatest

137

thinkers and innovators sank into lives of chronic illness as a result of simple ecological and dietary imbalance. The seed of this trend is evident in the Renaissance, as price, novelty, capital, and other material considerations began to displace worth, truth, spirit, and other nonmaterial values.

"*Quod me nutrit me destruit.*" What nourishes me destroys me—Marlowe's motto—is one of the basic laws of change. Yin changes into yang; yang changes into yin. Our desire, our goal, our dream in life ultimately turns into its opposite and consumes us. Leonardo's quest for knowledge led him to conceive of weapons of mass destruction. Columbus' unswerving determination to reach Cathay and reap the gold of the East led to his downfall and humiliation. Marlowe's reckless devotion to the muse of poetry and freedom to express his innermost thoughts nearly cost him his life.

Leonardo, the apostle of light, was enveloped by darkness. Columbus, the admiral of the ocean sea, was swallowed by space. The young Marlowe/Shakespeare, as the Sonnets attest, was obsessed with the ravages of time. Only the mature poet and playwright attained supreme consciousness and, if our reading of the *I Ching* is right, found lasting happiness. Every passage of his verse perfectly balances yin and yang, and like Yahweh in the Book of Job he dwarfs all critics. He is the Lao Tzu of the West. And like the Taoist sage, he renounced fame, fortune, and name and disappeared into a sublime void that contains and embraces all.

Living in the shadow of religious inquisition, Leonardo, Columbus, and Marlowe/Shakespeare were all dependent on wealthy patrons for their livelihood, and each sacrificed his muse to retain their favor. But the gifts of the heart they bequeathed us—the world's most beautiful art and literature, the endless dream of a new heaven on earth beyond the horizon, a world of enduring health and peace—survive, inspiring us to greater heights as the Spiral of Life continues to unfold. ❖

# Appendices

## I. Physiognomy

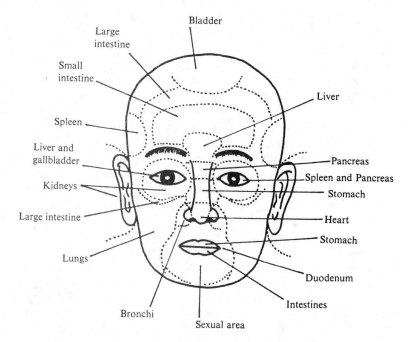

### Further Reading

Michio Kushi, *How to See Your Health: The Book of Oriental Diagnosis,* Japan Publications, 1986. The most complete text available on Oriental diagnosis.

Michio Kushi, *Your Face Never Lies,* Avery Publications, 1983. A brief introduction to Oriental diagnosis.

Michio Kushi and Alex Jack, *The Gospel of Peace: Jesus's Teachings of Eternal Truth* (Japan Publications, 1992). Study of the long-lost Gospel of Thomas, including Jesus' character and personality.

Alex Jack, *Inspector Ginkgo Tips His Hat to Sherlock Holmes,* One Peaceful World Press, 1994. Novel with a macrobiotic detective who uses Oriental diagnosis to solve his cases; includes study of Sherlock Holmes.

# II. Five Transformations and Nine Star Ki

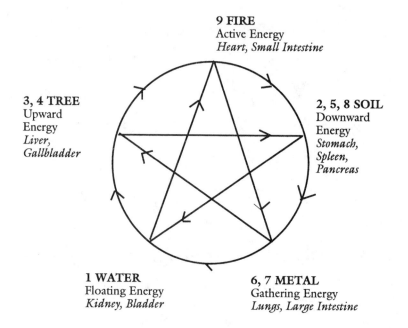

**9 FIRE**
Active Energy
*Heart, Small Intestine*

**3, 4 TREE**
Upward
Energy
*Liver,
Gallbladder*

**2, 5, 8 SOIL**
Downward
Energy
*Stomach,
Spleen,
Pancreas*

**1 WATER**
Floating Energy
*Kidney, Bladder*

**6, 7 METAL**
Gathering Energy
*Lungs, Large Intestine*

## The Two Cycles of Energy Flow

The outer clockwise direction indicates the Nourishing Cycle of energy flow and shows how adjacent energies support each other. For example, tree nourishes fire; fire nourishes soil; soil nourishes metal; and so on. The inner starlike direction shows the Regulating Cycle. Tree suppresses soil; soil dams water; water extin-guishes fire; fire melts metal; metal cuts tree.

## How to Calculate the Years

The basic Nine Star Ki cycle repeats every nine years. To calculate the energy of any year, add all four digits, reduce to a single digit, and subtract from 11. For example, 1995 = 24 = 6; 11 - 6 = 5. 1995 is a 5 year. Or take 1492. 1492 = 16 = 7; 11-7 = 4. Remember, the Nine Star Ki year begins on February 4, so dates between January 1 and February 3 are counted as part of the previous year.

# The Nine-Year Cycle

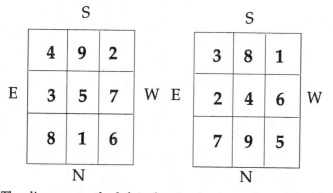

The diagram on the left is the standard arrangement with 5 in the center and the other numbers also in their home spot. The diagram on the right represents the next year (or month). Note each number moves forward, e.g., 1 in the north moves to the 2 spot in the southwest. There are seven other basic cycles through which the numbers spiral until they return home.

# The 81-Year Cycle

The 81-Year Cycle governs periods of time spanning several generations. The chart lists the 81-year-cycles of the modern era:

| | | | |
|---|---|---|---|
| #9 | 1226-1307 | Age of Chivalry | Dante, Marco Polo |
| #8 | 1307-1388 | Decline of Middle Ages | Tamburlaine |
| #7 | 1388-1469 | Early Renaissance | Chaucer, Gutenburg |
| #6 | 1469-1550 | Age of Discovery | Leonardo, Columbus |
| #5 | 1550-1631 | Age of Reformation | Shakespeare, Galileo |
| #4 | 1631-1712 | The Enlightenment | Descartes, Newton |
| #3 | 1712-1793 | Age of Democracy | Franklin, Jefferson |
| #2 | 1793-1874 | Industrial Revolution | Darwin, Marx |
| #1 | 1874-1955 | Age of Science and Medicine | Pasteur, Freud, Einstein |
| | | Age of Ideology | Hitler, Mao, Gandhi |
| #9 | 1955-2036 | Age of Natural Health | Ohsawa, Kushi |
| #8 | 2036-2117 | New Scientific Revolution | |
| #7 | 2117- | New Era of Humanity | |

# Further Reading

Michio Kushi and Edward Esko, *Nine Star Ki*, One Peaceful World Press, 1991. Indispensable handbook.

# III. *I Ching*

Fu Hi, the legendary ruler of ancient China, introduced the law of change by formulating the language of yin and yang. He expressed these polar tendencies as a solid line (—) for yang, Heaven's Force, and a broken line (- -) for yin, Earth's force. With this very simple system, he was able to describe the universal cycle of change that governs all things. Later, Fu Hi's eight trigrams were expanded into 64 hexagrams, and this became the basis for the *I Ching* or *The Book of Change*.

## Correspondence with the Bible

The story of the Flood and how the animals entered Noah's ark two by two is a universal parable dealing with the survival of life on earth and the coming of a new epoch. The animals in Noah's ship represent all the pairs of complementary opposites in our world. An elephant, for example, is large, a mouse is small. A camel is crooked, a horse is straight. A lion is strong, a lamb is weak. A bird flies high, a snake crawls low. The ark is a place in which all of the opposites that constitute the world exist in peace and harmony with one another.

The Flood story appears to have no Oriental counterpart. But if we look carefully at the arrangement of the *I Ching*, we find the same mythic structure. The basic elements of the ancient *Book of Change* are eight trigrams signifying Heaven and Earth, Thunder and Wind, Water and Fire, and Mountain and Lake. The eight trigrams are also known as the Father and Mother, the Eldest Son and Eldest Daughter, the Middle Son and Middle Daughter, and the Youngest Son and Youngest Daughter. These designations corresond with the eight persons in the ark: Noah and his wife, their three sons, and the sons' three wives. According to legend, Fu Hi, the legendary culture bearer and first emperor of China, copied these hexagrams from the markings on the back of a giant tortoise which surfaced following a great inundation of the Lo River. From the eight trigrams, sixty-four hexagrams are formed, which with their several thousand permutations parallel the vast menagerie of birds and animals in the ark. Later, the primordial vessel and its

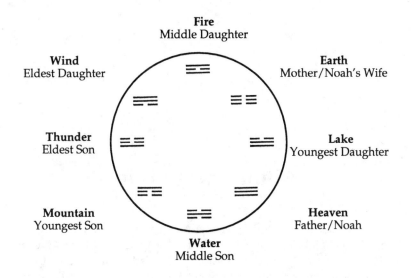

**Fire**
Middle Daughter

**Wind**
Eldest Daughter

**Earth**
Mother/Noah's Wife

**Thunder**
Eldest Son

**Lake**
Youngest Daughter

**Mountain**
Youngest Son

**Heaven**
Father/Noah

**Water**
Middle Son

eight inhabitants turn up in Buddhist symbolism as the Noble Eightfold Path and raft to the far shore of Nirvana.

Although Noah's ark resembles a physical craft, it primarily signifies a spiritual orientation toward the world. The Flood comes when we separate opposites into moral categories and see things in terms of good and evil, holy and impure, sacred and profane, rather than experiencing our existence as a unified whole. By provisioning our minds with as many pairs of mutually supportive opposites as we can accomodate, we build up our capacity to withstand the waters rising ominously around us and to live a larger life *(macro bios)*. By nourishing all the energies in the storehold of our consciousness, we acquire the ability to sail over any situation, however threatening. By skillfully combining pairs of opposites as Noah did by releasing the raven of the intellect and the dove of intuition, we shall reach high ground. The primal waters of ignorance and unconsciousness will recede. With our families, we can dock our ark between the summits of extreme yin and yang and disembark into a radiant new world.

*This excerpt is from an article "Rebuilding the Ark" by Alex Jack that appeared in the* East West Journal *in January, 1980.*

## Further Reading

Richard Wilhelm, *I Ching*, Princeton University Press, 1950, 1967. The most authoritative English translation, including Confucius' commentary.

# About the Author

Alex Jack was born in Chicago in 1945 and grew up in Evanston, Illinois, and Scarsdale, New York. He graduated from Oberlin College with a degree in philosophy, studied for a year in India, and reported on the war in Vietnam. For nearly thirty years he has been involved in spreading the diet and health revolution, traveling and teaching in China, Japan, Russia, Europe, and throughout North America. During this time, he served as editor-in-chief of the *East West Journal*, general manager of the Kushi Institute, director of the One Peaceful World Society, and a macrobiotic teacher and counselor.

Alex teaches health care and philosophy at the Kushi Institute in Becket, Massachusetts, and is the author several books including *The Cancer-Prevention Diet, Diet for a Strong Heart,* and *AIDS and Beyond* (with Michio Kushi); *The Complete Guide to Macrobiotic Cooking* (with Aveline Kushi); *Promenade Home* and *Amber Waves of Grain* (with Gale Jack); *Let Food Be Thy Medicine; Out of Thin Air: A Satire on Owls and Ozone, Beef and Biodiversity, and Grains and Global Warming;* and *Inspector Ginkgo Tips His Hat to Sherlock Holmes..*

He lives with his wife Gale, a cooking teacher, and his daughter, Masha. He is presently editing his father's autobiography and preparing the next volume of *Profiles in Oriental Diagnosis.*